MASTERCHEF

MASTERCHEF

Compiled by Philippa Robinson
Edited by Kelly Davis

BBC BOOKS

MasterChef
A Union Pictures production for the BBC
Series devised by Franc Roddam
Executive Producer: Bradley Adams
Producer: Philippa Robinson
Director: Richard Bryan

Book compiled by Philippa Robinson
Photography by Paul Kemp
Home Economist: Nicola Diggins
Stylist: Jane Kemp
Designer: Bill Mason
With special thanks to Carole Townsend and Miranda McMinn
Published by BBC Books
A division of BBC Enterprises Ltd
Woodlands, 80 Wood Lane, London W12 0TT

Typeset in Great Britain in Caslon by Ace Filmsetting Ltd, Frome, Somerset
Colour printed in Great Britain by Lawrence Allen Ltd, Weston-super-Mare, Somerset
Printed and bound in England by St Ives plc, Richard Clay Ltd, England

CONTENTS

Living in Hollywood and travelling around the world, I have often found myself defending British cooking in the face of ill-informed criticism. I have always tried to convince detractors that in the homes of Britain there is a style and class of cooking, a mixture of both traditional and modern influences, that can match any cuisine the world has to offer. It was this that inspired me to develop the idea of *MasterChef*.

FRANC RODDAM, creator of *MasterChef*

Note to the Reader

For anyone who missed the *MasterChef* programmes on TV, it seems a good idea to outline the basic rules of the competition. Each competitor was expected to cook a three-course meal for four people within 2½ hours. The total amount spent on the ingredients had to be £30 or less, and each contestant was allowed to bring a maximum of five items from home and one partly prepared in advance (e.g. stock or marinade).

In this book we have begun with a chapter on the 27 contestants, listed in alphabetical order. This is followed by the menus and recipes from the final, semi-final and regional heats. One point worth noting: because the time available in the competition was limited, certain dishes have been cooked faster and at a higher temperature than usual. In the case of meringues, for example, you may wish to bake them for longer in a cooler oven in order to avoid browning. In addition, some contestants chose to use very unusual ingredients which are only available in certain specialist shops. In such cases, we have tried to suggest more common alternatives.

So it only remains to say, 'Happy cooking!' We hope you enjoy re-living the excitement of the competition and trying the many varied and delicious recipes submitted by our talented contestants.

PHILIPPA ROBINSON, Producer

Foreword

At the end of the first day's cooking, Michael Caine, Richard Shepherd and I retired to consider the efforts of our three contestants. We deliberated in silence for a few minutes.

Michael was the first to speak up: 'I would have been happy to pay to eat any of it.' Richard and I agreed enthusiastically and indeed our most persistent problem in judging, and most consistent delight in tasting, was the very high standard of cooking practised by all our competitors. So high was the standard that our supposedly decorous and judicial 'tastings' quickly degenerated into fully fledged 'eatings'. Sir Terence Conran's kidnapping of a dish of roast potatoes wasn't the only time that a judge murmured something along the lines of 'I really must just have one more little taste of this.'

When Franc Roddam, Brad Adams and I first discussed the series – this was about a year before we went into the studio – we had a hunch that this country might produce some of the best amateur cooks in the world. There is a food revolution going on in Britain. It began, I suppose, when the sunny cookery books of Elizabeth David brightened the last years of post-war rationing; gained momentum when the newspaper colour supplements chose to devote considerable space to food and cookery (based on the obvious assumptions that everyone likes to eat and that good food looks glamorous and colourful); and began to reach its widest audience when the development of cheap foreign travel allowed millions of people to taste what was going on out there in France, in the Mediterranean and most recently in South-East Asia. And of course television spread the word as well.

MasterChef and today's other cookery programmes (increasing as you will have noticed in quantity and quality) are the latest in a celebrated line beginning with Philip Harbin and progressing via Fanny Craddock, Graham Kerr and Delia Smith. Couple this rapidly growing popular interest in good food with the glorious tradition of British amateurism – remember that throughout history our amateurs have often been superior to other country's professionals – and it seemed a pretty sure thing that I was going to eat rather well during our search for the best amateur cook in Great Britain.

We advertised modestly but widely for contestants in a few well-chosen national newspapers and magazines. There were also a number of radio interviews ranging from local radio to the *Gloria Hunniford Show* on Radio 2, as well as thousands of notices placed in food shops across the country. Would-be contestants were required to fill in an application form of staggering depth and complexity – our applicants ranged from clergymen to schoolchildren to jet fighter pilots to deep sea divers. There were as many men as women. A rigorous series of regional cook-offs followed: 27 champions of the kitchen emerged to face the final judges and the cameras. They cooked like angels, unfazed by the distractions of lights, cables, cameras and judges poking their fingers into dishes and asking generally irritating questions such as 'What's that?'

In all cases what emerged from the kitchens showed a great knowledge of the state of the art of cookery and a refreshingly instinctive feel for good food which we sometimes fear isn't to be found on this side of the Channel. There was a blessed absence of gimmickry, a deft use of what were once considered exotic ingredients – saffron, balsamic vinegar, samphire – and often bold reworkings of traditional British culinary themes. It will not surprise anyone to hear that never have so many brilliant puddings been prepared for such a happy few. All the judges – chefs and notable food lovers alike – agreed that the nation's appetites were in safe hands.

LOYD GROSSMAN

The Contestants

JANET AITKEN

'I have a passion for wonderful food. There is very little that is more pleasurable than sharing a special meal with a husband, wife or close friend,' says Janet. Despite her busy job as manageress of a newsagent's in Reading she still finds time to entertain lavishly. 'One of the things I really love to do is have "theme evenings" with my husband Stuart and daughter Leila. I cook a meal – something like Indian, Chinese, Spanish or Greek – and we all dress up accordingly and eat our meal accompanied by the appropriate music.' A barbecue enthusiast, she never travels without her trusty saucepan and believes that the best way to eat is outside. 'I love putting the holiday feel into meals when I'm entertaining and even our holidays themselves are dictated by food.'

CAROL ALEXANDER

Having studied fashion design at art college, Carol progressed to interior design and now owns a natural beauty store with her mother in Cumbria. 'I have a bit of a butterfly brain and I like to flit from one thing to another, although my real ambition is one day to own a country house hotel in the Lake District so I could combine my interior design with my love of cooking.' Entertaining is her forte and she barely needs an excuse to cook for a party.

ROBERT ASH

For Robert Ash, jazz musician and house husband, cooking is more than a creative hobby, it's a science. His interest in food has drawn him to different cities around the world and he likens the way he now approaches food to the way other people look at architecture: How has it been constructed? Why does it work? He is an improvisational chef who rarely uses recipe books. Recently he has found inspiration in the recipes produced in the nineteenth century by the chefs of gentlemen's clubs, who sought to outdo each other's culinary feats. He is currently researching the life of Alexis Soyer, one-time chef at the Reform Club, and hopes to find enough material to write his biography. His own philosophy of cooking is that a dish with really good basic ingredients is impossible to ruin. 'I can burn it,' he says, 'but that's something else.'

MARTIN BENTON

Martin is a computer systems analyst from Cardiff whose hobbies include fantasy board games such as Dungeons and Dragons, as well as motorcycling. But his real passion is cooking. He and his wife, Anne, devote each weekend to devising new recipes, buying and preparing the food and finally sitting down to eat and enjoy the fruits of their labour. Martin says, 'We cook as a husband and wife team. All the recipes and tastes I make are designed by both of us although I'm better at actually doing it. I'm very much influenced by modern European cooking at the moment, in particular Freddy Girardet's "Cuisine Spontanée". It's the book I'd take to a desert island. I also believe firmly that in cooking there's no substitute for butter, cream and red meat.'

JOAN BUNTING

Joan is a co-ordinator for hospital and home tuition in North Tyneside where she and her husband, both confirmed Francophiles, teach wine appreciation evening classes at the University of Newcastle. Her favourite wines come from the Rhône and Provence. 'My ambition is to run food and wine holidays in France where we could teach guests to cook and sample the regional dishes as well as explore the local markets for delicious fresh produce.' Of her own culinary style she says, 'I come from a family with a tradition of good honest cooking. My grandmother, who was a wonderful cook, started me off when I was only two.'

SUSAN COWLEY

Susan is head teacher at Birmingham Children's Hospital. She lives with her husband, two children and two huge rabbits, Fat Bun and Speckledy, in a haunted Georgian house which they've been renovating since they bought it eleven years ago. 'I love looking at old recipes as they seem to have some meaning if you live in an old house – you can relate them to the four walls around you. I can think, "This might have been eaten here before!" I enjoy making old-fashioned recipes because I enjoy doing things from scratch. Recipes that make life easier don't have the same satisfaction. I like my cooking to be a little bit difficult!' However, Susan does admit, 'I'm a messy cook without a doubt. No matter how good my intentions are when I start out, I always get to some crisis point and the kitchen turns into chaos.'

SILVIJA DAVIDSON

Silvija Davidson works for The International Wine & Food Society, writes the occasional cookery article, and also finds time to enjoy the theatre. Her interest in cookery initially arose out of desperation – caught as she was between ghastly food at school and endless Latvian soup at home! Her low boredom threshold means that she is constantly re-inventing dishes and literally dreaming up new culinary combinations. She is particularly interested in organic food and rare-breed meat from animals reared as naturally as possible. Having taught herself from cookbooks, she believes that anyone else can do the same.

MARY FERRIS

Mary is a freelance PR consultant, and also works with the Samaritans, helping to recruit volunteers. Since moving to Wales from London she has had time to be more adventurous in what she cooks, and has discovered the joys of local produce and what she calls 'pickings from hedgerows'. She comes from a large family where 'everybody had to do their bit', so she is undaunted by cooking for large numbers. Not surprisingly, the kitchen is the focal point of her house, and she admits that, as the chef, she enjoys 'being centre-stage', and aims to impress family and guests with a 'flamboyant end result'.

TONY FITZWILLIAM-PIPE

Tony is a probation officer at Strangeways, and is also studying for a Master's Degree in computing at Lancaster University. A keen weight-lifter, he is interested in healthy eating and cooking with very little fat. He learned by watching his mother, an excellent cook, but he cannot bear company in the kitchen himself, preferring to remain in control from start to finish. He harbours no secret desire to open his own restaurant: 'My parents were publicans and I know what a crippling job it can be. Far too much like hard work.' He has, however, been considering working on a computerised recipe book, for which he believes there is a definite market.

LILY GIBB

Lily's late husband was the Head Gamekeeper on the Hunthill Estate near Angus and she has lived in Glen Lethnot, where she's an active member of the Scottish Women's Rural Institute, since her marriage in 1942. Before that she lived nearby on her parents' farm. 'I was fortunate to be a farmer's daughter during wartime. I was about fourteen and mother was too busy outside rearing chickens to have much time for the house, so I took over the household, and I've been cooking ever since.' Lily thoroughly enjoys experimenting with new recipes but adds, 'If I was marooned on a desert island Constance Spry is the only book I would want with me.'

JANE GLENCROSS

Jane lives in Newport and works in Cardiff, where she teaches four- to five-year-olds in an independent school. She writes poetry and enjoys dress-making. But her favourite hobby is cooking, which she does to relax, often with her fiancé. She enjoys experimenting, using techniques from cookery books to create her own recipes. She would love to have a bistro with live folk music and dishes from all over the world. She is extremely fond of spices, and admits, 'We are even taking our Indian spices on our honeymoon with us!'

BRIAN GLOVER

Brian is a librarian at Exeter University with a Ph.D. in Medieval English poetry. He was brought up on a farm in Lancashire where he was taught to cook as a child by his grandmother, who was an 'excellent plain farmhouse cook'. However, rebellion came in his teenage years: 'I was fond of American cookbooks which meant I would produce elaborate confections, almost bankrupting my mother in the process.' He's more level-headed now, preferring fish and vegetables which he cooks simply to bring out their innate qualities. Brian would like to develop his love of food and cooking into a career as a food writer.

ANTHONY HAROLD

When he is not tap-dancing, or conjuring up new dishes, Anthony is studying for his GCSEs although he admits, 'I live, sleep and think food.' His practical interest in cooking began when he was four, and for the last five years he has cooked for his family every day – he doesn't allow his mother in the kitchen! Extremely modest about his precocious talent, he claims, 'I cook because there are not a lot of other things I can do because of my immunity deficiency.' His ambition is to have his own cookery programme, and he plans to open his own hotel and restaurant one day, preferably in Devon.

MARY HENDRY

Mary lives in Northamptonshire where she helps her husband with his busy architectural practice and still finds time to fund-raise for the local branch of the National Children's Home, help with Riding for the Disabled and deliver Meals on Wheels. Food is her passion, particularly good healthy food, although she admits that this hasn't always been the case. 'The first meal that I cooked for my husband nearly killed him off, but luckily for both of us I've improved considerably since my early days in the kitchen. The wonderful thing about cooking is that you can never stop learning. I'm constantly on the lookout for new recipes. I even tuck myself up in bed at night with a cookery book the way other people read novels.'

PAM HOLMES

Pam describes herself as a Leicester City football supporter and crossword fanatic. She and her husband live in a village near Lincoln with Rosie their golden retriever and Jason the bald parrot. The kitchen is her favourite room in the house and she spends as much time there as she can. 'I love to cook. I'd rather cook than anything else. I cook dinner every evening that we're home and I do all my own baking and jam-making. I cook every type of food I can, from traditional English to curries, although we always have a roast on Sundays.' An avid reader and collector of cookbooks, she makes a beeline for the cookery shelf whenever she enters a bookshop.

KIERAN McBRIDE

Eighteen-year-old Kieran, who has just finished a hotel catering course at Kirby College, learned to cook by watching his mum. He won his first competition aged ten, beating five adults. At the age of twelve he became the Junior Cook of the North-East, and in the process picked up some advice from John Tovey, who accused him of being 'a right mucky worker'. 'That completely changed me,' he admits. 'Now I clear up as I go along!' He satisfies his creative urges and his sweet tooth by making exotic desserts, and recommends that amateur cooks avoid becoming too serious: 'It's only cooking and it's meant to be fun.'

OLGA MORPETH

As well as cooking, Olga teaches flower-arranging, keeps bees and collects unusual plants for her large garden. She began to cook when she was twelve, and first experimented with cakes and lemon meringue pies. Even now she adores making gateaux, and eating them too when her conscience doesn't get the better of her. Her entire family is vegetarian, and although she occasionally gets a little frustrated at the limitations imposed by cooking without meat, she says that she could no longer bring herself to cook pork or beef. She thoroughly enjoys compiling new and unusual recipes and friends travelling to London are always dispatched to find exotic ingredients – such as sun-dried tomatoes or balsamic vinegar – which she finds hard to track down in Middlesbrough.

KATY MORSE

Katy is the postwoman in Portscatho, Cornwall. Her reason for cooking is simple: 'I love food and I live to eat.' Past culinary triumphs have included Spanish and Chinese evenings. During the summer months Katy practises her cooking in the caravan that she shares with her husband, Lionel, and their Jack Russell, Shep. Given the opportunity she would love to have a little bistro, which would be a 'casual, interesting' affair, with a varied price range and a constantly changing 'specials' blackboard.

MARY OSWELL

Mary describes herself as a 'distraught, disorganised housewife', but she is also a freelance technical writer, and caters for bed and breakfast guests in the family's beautiful Northumberland home. She was originally inspired by a Robert Carrier article thirty years ago, but her special interest these days is Middle and Far Eastern food – her husband lived in Malaysia as a child, and they have visited there several times. She draws a distinction between cooking for guests, which is fun and relaxing, and for the family, which with three children underfoot tends to be rather rushed and not quite so pleasurable. Nevertheless, she enjoys extending her culinary skills to invent new dishes for her baby daughter, Katie, who is no doubt delighted to act as guinea-pig.

GRAEME RICHARDSON

Several years of eating out in restaurants have convinced Graeme, a London-based fashion photographer, that home-cooked food is cheaper and tastier. Monkfish in chocolate and chilli is only one of the unusual dishes you're likely to enjoy at his home. He dislikes 'trendy' food, but finds traditional cooking too fatty, so he bows to modernity by removing all fat before cooking. He claims that his interest in cooking began one day when, as a poor student, he was fishing off Bournemouth Pier. To his amazement he landed a huge catch and was then obliged to buy a book to find out what to do with all the fish. He hasn't looked back since. However, in a rash moment, he reveals the truth behind his talent: 'I cook because my wife doesn't – it's a bit of a disaster when she does!'

ALISON RIDDELL

As well as being actively involved in conservation and editing her ski club magazine, Alison grows vegetables and herbs, keeps bees for their honey, and takes her dog, Rhubarb, for walks in the New Forest, where she collects wild fungi, elderflowers, and blackberries, all of which find their way into her cooking. 'It's fun going for a walk,' she says, 'and if you find something to cook it is even more enjoyable.' She learned all the basics from her mother who was a good cook, and she is especially good at preparing meals in a hurry, occasionally catering for large numbers. Her inspiration often arrives in the middle of the night, and so she can sometimes be found burning the midnight oil, penning new recipes.

RACHEL RUTTER

Rachel and her husband run a dairy farm in Cheshire, and when she is not attending to their pedigree Friesians, she is kept occupied by the local sugarcraft guild of which she is a founder member. She is particularly interested in how recipes have developed over the centuries. Her favourite example is a Roman recipe for cooking flamingo or parrot, although she thinks there's probably not much call for this dish in her part of the world. Her family have traditional tastes: 'Meat and two veg must look like meat and two veg. And, being hard-working farmers, the portions have to be substantial.' However, her artistic side comes into its own when she makes cakes and desserts.

PETER SAYERS

Peter lives in Cheltenham where he can usually be found either in the kitchen or in his workshop making 'anything that comes along', from ornate wooden jewel boxes to a small rocking chair for his grandson. Having learned to cook at his mother's side in the difficult years of rationing he is now teaching his grandchildren the basics – how to make pancakes, buns, biscuits and cakes. Since he retired he has had plenty of time to cook as well as travel, going to Europe on caravanning holidays with his wife and picking up new recipes along the way. He relishes other people's enjoyment of his cooking, and declares, 'I aim to achieve a professional standard at all times.'

MIKE SILVERSTONE

Mike is a medical laboratory scientific officer in a busy haematology department in Chesterfield. Since taking up cooking seriously five years ago, he has become something of a culinary agony aunt to his friends, who come to him with all their 'cooking problems'. As well as being a music lover, theatre-goer and a keen organic gardener, he is studying for an MSc in Biomedical Sciences. When his exams are over, he is considering doing some catering for professional dinner parties, which would be a step towards his dream of 'giving everything up and opening a little restaurant of my own'.

ALAN SIM

'I'm a slut in the kitchen,' says Alan Sim. Originally from Ayrshire, he has been seduced by the charms of Dorset where he works as a vet. It seems that when he falls, he falls heavily. While at university he decided he had better learn to cook. He went to a nearby bookshop, picked up Elizabeth David's *French Provincial Cooking*, and 'that was it, I was hooked. It's the first cookery book I ever owned and it's still the best.' And Alan should know. He has about 350 other cookery books to compare it with. For him, one of the greatest joys is a silent dinner table: 'I love to see everyone pigging into my food, too busy eating to talk.'

FRANCES SMITH

Frances and her husband, Neil, grow vegetables and herbs for the restaurant and catering trade. They specialise in unusual salad leaves, growing up to 300 different plants, and they also keep quail and guinea fowl. Living 6 miles from the nearest town, Frances often has to improvise in her cooking, which she finds an enjoyable challenge, drawing inspiration from her mother who brought her up during post-war rationing and was always creating 'wonderful meals out of nothing'. She loves using fruit, vegetables and herbs from the garden, and her approach to creating an excellent meal is to 'buy the best ingredients I can afford and make sure I do nothing to spoil them'. She cooks for relaxation, adding, 'I only cook for love, I could never do it for money.'

RICHARD SUTTON

Richard is a district nurse in Leeds with an all-consuming passion for cooking. He and his wife, Caroline, enjoy trying out the cosmopolitan restaurants in their area, ranging from Chinese to Mexican. Sometimes Richard will adapt – but not copy – certain elements of these culinary styles when entertaining, which he does often. He loves to 'give other people the pleasure of eating what I produce'. A self-critical perfectionist, he began cooking at an early age, and believes he might have become professional had his artistic talent not been suppressed. He remains a highly informed amateur, and still cherishes a dream of opening a small unpretentious bistro. Caroline, whose gastronomic pleasure is tempered by the washing up, 'reckons she needs a dishwasher to keep up with me,' he says.

THE FINAL

The Winner

JOAN BUNTING'S MENU

·

STARTER
Mussels with pistou
·
MAIN COURSE
Quails with couscous
Spring cabbage with garlic
and juniper
·
DESSERT
Mediterranean islands

Mussels with pistou

Pistou is a classic Provençal mix
which you can use in soups and
pastas, but if you don't like garlic
don't make this! The garlic, basil
and oil must be ground in a pestle
and mortar. Although it's a lengthy
process it really makes a difference
to the end result.

'Rustic, straightforward and honest.'
ANTON MOSIMANN

2 lb (1 kg) fresh mussels, scrubbed and
bearded
5 fl oz (150 ml) dry white wine
3 cloves garlic
10 sprigs of very fresh basil
2–3 tablespoons olive oil
Salt and pepper
Rock salt (optional)

Put the mussels in a pan with the
wine and place over a moderate heat
until most of the shells have opened.
Discard any unopened mussels, drain
the rest and remove the empty half
shells. In a mortar, pound the garlic
and basil until smooth (this can be
started in a food processor if you
wish). Add the olive oil drop by drop
until the mixture forms a smooth
paste. Season to taste with salt and
pepper, add a little pistou to each half
mussel and heat briefly under a hot
grill. Set the mussels on a layer of rock
salt to serve, if you wish.

Quails with couscous

This is based on a Moroccan dish in which pigeons rather than quails are used. Using either squabs or poussins would be a cheaper alternative to quails and would be almost as good. Keep testing the birds when they're cooking – it's essential not to overcook them.

1 tablespoon olive oil or melted butter
Salt
8 oz (225 g) couscous
2–3 tablespoons pine nuts, toasted
2–3 oz (50–75 g) large plump raisins, soaked in Armagnac
4 pairs quails
8 rashers bacon
A little red wine
Pepper
A few sprigs of fresh coriander or parsley, to garnish

Put 10 fl oz (300 ml) water and 1 tablespoon olive oil or butter in a large saucepan. Add a pinch of salt and bring to the boil. Remove from the heat, add the couscous, stir and leave to swell for 15 minutes. Stir again and add the pine nuts and raisins. Stuff the quails with some of the couscous mixture, and secure with cocktail sticks. Cover each quail with bacon and place in a roasting dish. Pour in a little red wine and season with salt and pepper. Bake for 8–10 minutes at gas mark 7–8, 425–450°F (220–230°C), until very tender. Strain the sauce and serve separately. Pile the reheated remaining couscous in the centre of a suitable dish and surround with the quails. Pour over the sauce and garnish with coriander or parsley.

Spring cabbage with garlic and juniper

This is a Delia Smith recipe which I've adapted by adding more garlic and olive oil. Cut the cabbage very finely indeed. You *must* use a sparkling fresh cabbage, not a dreary old one. The cabbage I used for the *MasterChef* competition came fresh from my father's allotment.

1 head fresh spring cabbage
2 tablespoons olive oil
2 cloves garlic, crushed
2 shallots, finely chopped
6 juniper berries, crushed
Salt and pepper

Shred the cabbage very finely, then place in a colander and wash and drain thoroughly. Heat the oil in a heavy-based pan and sauté the garlic and shallots until tender. Turn the cabbage in the oil until it is well coated. Then place in a casserole with the crushed juniper berries. Season with salt and pepper, place on the lowest shelf in the oven, and bake at gas mark 5, 375°F (190°C), for about 30 minutes, stirring once or twice.

Mediterranean islands

This is a classic French recipe and a favourite of both my son and my mother. When I cook a meal as a treat, my mother always says, 'Make that thing with the meringues floating on top.'

1 pint (600 ml) full cream milk
1 vanilla pod
3 large fresh eggs, separated
4–5 tablespoons caster sugar
1 tablespoon rum, or orange liqueur
4 oz (100 g) granulated sugar
1 oz (25 g) almonds, chopped and toasted
Fresh fruit, to garnish

In a large frying pan, warm the milk with the vanilla pod. Beat the egg whites in a bowl until stiff, then add 3 tablespoons caster sugar. Poach spoonfuls of the meringue mixture in the hot milk until fluffy but firm. Slide on to a large plate. Now beat the egg yolks with the remaining caster sugar. Blend in the strained vanilla-flavoured milk and cook gently until the custard coats a spoon. Add the rum or liqueur. Leave to cool in a serving dish. To serve, float the 'islands' on the custard. Melt the granulated sugar in 4 fl oz (120 ml) water and boil until caramelised. Stir in the toasted almonds and drizzle over the 'islands'. Decorate with small pieces of fresh fruit.

BRIAN GLOVER'S MENU

·
STARTER
Grilled polenta with tapenade and goat's cheese
·
MAIN COURSE
Fillets of salmon with a hot salmon mousse and a sorrel sauce
Courgettes in tomato and chive butter
New potatoes with dill and lemon
·
DESSERT
Wood strawberry tartlets with bayleaf custard

Grilled polenta with tapenade and goat's cheese

Polenta is quite tricky, and you must make sure that it's lump-free. It helps to sift the polenta into the boiling water using your hand. Once made, it is an ideal base for strong-flavoured toppings.

'Wonderfully simple – upmarket peasant food.'
SIR ROY STRONG

FOR THE POLENTA
2–3 teaspoons salt
10 oz (275 g) polenta meal
Olive oil

FOR THE TAPENADE
4 oz (100 g) black olives, stoned
1 clove garlic, crushed
4 teaspoons capers
2 oz (50 g) good-quality tinned tuna fish in oil, drained and flaked
6 tinned fillets anchovies
2 tablespoons chopped fresh basil

4 oz (100 g) goat's cheese
A little olive oil

FOR THE SALAD AND DRESSING
3 tablespoons olive oil
2 teaspoons red wine vinegar
½ teaspoon French mustard
1 tablespoon chopped fresh basil
1 clove garlic, halved
Salt and black pepper
4 oz (100 g) rocket and lettuce leaves, mixed

To make the polenta, bring 3 pints (1.75 litres) water to the boil in a large saucepan with the salt. When boiling, adjust the heat to a simmer and, stirring all the time, gradually add the polenta meal in a constant stream, avoiding lumps. When all the polenta is in, cook gently, stirring almost constantly for 45 minutes. Taste and add more salt if necessary. Oil a 1 in (2.5 cm) deep 9 × 12 in (23 × 30 cm) baking tray. Pour in the polenta, smooth out and leave for 3–4 hours to cool and set.

For the tapenade, simply whiz all the ingredients in a food processor or blender until they form a paste. Alternatively, pound the olives, garlic and capers in a mortar until they form a paste. Then work in the tuna, anchovies, and lastly the basil.

For the salad, mix together the dressing ingredients and allow to stand for 1 hour. Remove the garlic. Just before serving, toss the salad with the dressing.

To assemble the dish, turn out the polenta and cut out 4 × 2 in (5 cm) circles or squares. Slice each of these in half horizontally. Arrange on foil under a hot grill for 5–10 minutes until the edges begin to brown. Spread with tapenade, top with rinded and thinly sliced goat's cheese, drizzle over some olive oil, and grill for 3 more minutes. Serve with a little salad.

Fillets of salmon with a hot salmon mousse and a sorrel sauce

it's worth getting wild salmon for this – it differs in texture as well as flavour. The sorrel sauce is a classic French accompaniment to fish and you could still have an excellent dish if you wanted to leave out the mousse.

'A wonderful sorrel sauce – it doesn't overwhelm.'
SIR ROY STRONG

1 × 3½ lb (1.5 kg) salmon, filleted and skinned
A little olive oil

FOR THE MOUSSE
1 egg white, chilled
7 fl oz (200 ml) double cream, chilled
Salt and cayenne pepper
Juice of ½ lemon
3 tablespoons chopped fresh dill

FOR THE SAUCE
1 shallot, peeled and chopped
2 oz (50 g) butter, chilled
3 fl oz (85 ml) vermouth
10 fl oz (300 ml) fish stock
1 handful fresh sorrel, shredded
2 fl oz (50 ml) double cream
Salt and pepper

Weigh the salmon fillets and remove 8 oz (225 g) from the ends and sides for the mousse. Cut the remainder into equal-sized slices across the fillet, 2–3 for each portion. Blend the 8 oz

(225 g) salmon in a food processor or blender until smooth, add the egg white and cream and blend again. Season quite strongly with salt, cayenne and lemon juice. Chill for at least 30 minutes. Line the bases of 4 ramekins with lightly buttered greaseproof paper. Divide half the mixture between the ramekins, sprinkle over the chopped dill and then top with the remaining salmon mixture. Cover each ramekin with foil and cook for 15 minutes in a shallow baking tray half filled with water at gas mark 5–6, 375–400°F (190–200°C). Keep warm and turn out just before serving.

For the sauce, fry the shallot in ½ oz (15 g) butter until soft. Add the vermouth and reduce rapidly until a few teaspoonsful remain. Now add the stock and reduce again, skimming from time to time. You should end up with just over 5 fl oz (150 ml) liquid to strain into a clean pan. Meanwhile, melt another ½ oz (15 g) butter in a pan, add almost all the shredded sorrel leaves and cook gently for a few minutes. Add to the sauce with the cream and reduce gently. Season to taste with salt and pepper. Finish by whisking in the remaining chilled butter and shredded sorrel.

Just before serving, fry the salmon fillets in a little olive oil for 1–2 minutes each side (or grill for 2–3 minutes each side). Then serve each fillet with a mousse and some sauce.

Courgettes in tomato and chive butter

2 oz (50 g) butter
1 bunch of fresh chives, finely chopped
1 tablespoon finely chopped fresh chervil
Salt and black pepper
8 oz (225 g) ripe tomatoes, skinned, seeded and cut into ¼ in (5 mm) dice
1 small red onion, finely chopped
1 lb (450 g) courgettes, cut into small dice

Cream 1 oz (25 g) butter with the chives, chervil, salt and black pepper. Gradually work in one-third of the tomatoes. Set aside. Melt the remaining butter in a pan and cook the onion slowly until soft. Add the courgettes and cook for about 5 minutes until tender. Do not allow to brown. Add the remaining tomatoes and cook for a further minute. Toss with the herb and tomato butter, and serve.

New potatoes with dill and lemon

This comes from an idea by Alice Waters, an American cook at the forefront of the Californian foodie movement. There is a real sense of event when your guests open the bag and steam pours out.

1½ lb (750 g) small potatoes, scraped
Salt and black pepper
3 tablespoons chopped fresh dill
1 tablespoon chopped fresh chives
Thinly pared rind of 1 lemon, cut into fine strips
4 tablespoons olive oil

Steam the potatoes over a pan of boiling water for 10 minutes. Fold 4 × 12 in (30 cm) circles of greaseproof paper in half and distribute the potatoes between them. Season with salt and black pepper, and sprinkle with the herbs and lemon rind. Drizzle over the olive oil – about 1 tablespoon per package. Fold over the paper and twist the edges to seal. Bake at gas mark 6, 400°F (200°C), for 30 minutes.

Wood strawberry tartlets with bayleaf custard

I'm fascinated by the history of food and I love searching out old recipes. I found the recipe for this bayleaf custard in a facsimile of an Elizabethan cookbook. If you can't get hold of crème fraîche you could try a mixture of double cream and yoghurt.

FOR THE PASTRY
4 oz (100 g) plain white flour
A pinch of salt
2 oz (50 g) caster sugar
3 oz (75 g) unsalted butter
2 oz (50 g) ground almonds
Grated rind and juice of ½ lemon
1 egg yolk

FOR THE FILLING AND GLAZE
4 tablespoons redcurrant jelly
1 tablespoon port
4 fl oz (120 ml) crème fraîche or a mixture of whipped cream and Greek yoghurt
1 punnet wood strawberries

FOR THE CUSTARD
10 fl oz (300 ml) single cream
3 fresh bayleaves, torn into pieces
½ vanilla pod
2 egg yolks
2 tablespoons vanilla-flavoured sugar
A few fresh bayleaves, to decorate

First make the pastry. Mix together the flour, salt and sugar and rub in the butter. Add the ground almonds and lemon rind. Bind with the egg yolk and lemon juice, then chill the pastry for 1 hour. Roll out and line 4 × 3 in (7.5 cm) tartlet tins. Bake blind at gas mark 5, 375°F (190°C), for 15 minutes until lightly browned.

For the glaze, melt the redcurrant jelly and port together. Allow to cool, then use some to brush the insides of the pastry cases. Divide the crème fraîche, or cream and yoghurt, between the 4 cases, arrange the fruit on top and brush with the remaining glaze.

For the custard, heat the cream in a small pan with the torn bayleaves and vanilla pod. Whisk together the egg yolks and sugar until pale. Whisk in the cream and heat in a bowl over a pan of simmering water until the custard thickens. Strain to remove the bayleaves and vanilla pod. Then serve the tartlets with the custard, decorated with a couple of fresh bayleaves.

SILVIJA DAVIDSON'S MENU

•

STARTER
Lakeland smoked eel with apple and potato pancake and a bacon and lime-dressed salad

•

MAIN COURSE
Scalloped beef platter
Pasta with cep and oyster mushroom sauce
Young carrots and fennel

•

DESSERT
Kent strawberry kissel with scented geranium meringue

Lakeland smoked eel with apple and potato pancake and a bacon and lime-dressed salad

In the *MasterChef* competition I used eel that was caught by my father and smoked by his cronies. I remember that even at the age of five I would quite happily strip off the skin and eat one in about 5 minutes. The pancakes are very versatile and if you left out the horseradish they'd go well with maple syrup and bacon, American breakfast style.

JOAN BUNTING'S FINAL MENU
Mussels with pistou, Quails with couscous, Spring cabbage with garlic and juniper,
Mediterranean islands

BRIAN GLOVER'S FINAL MENU
Grilled polenta with tapenade and goat's cheese, Fillets of salmon with a hot salmon mousse and a sorrel sauce, Courgettes in tomato and chive butter, New potatoes with dill and lemon, Wood strawberry tartlets with bayleaf custard

MASTERCHEF

BRIAN GLOVER'S SEMI-FINAL MENU
Salad of smoked trout and samphire with a tomato vinaigrette, Guineafowl marinated in
basil and olive oil, Turnip gratin, Cardamom cake with papaya and rhubarb

SILVIJA DAVIDSON'S SEMI-FINAL MENU
Crabmeat filo tarts, Gloucester pork roll with herb garden stuffing, Golden risotto,
Butter-tossed garden peas and cucumber, Soft cheese dumplings with a
fresh apricot sauce

MASTERCHEF

JOAN BUNTING'S SEMI-FINAL MENU
Salmon and asparagus mousse, Rack of Northumbrian lamb, Potato puffs, Provençal green beans, Summer fruit tartlets

BRIAN GLOVER'S MENU
Goat's cheese filos with salad and red pepper dressing, John Dory with a saffron and orange sauce, Spinach with nutmeg, Carrots with coriander, Caramelised pears with ginger and lime syllabub and walnut and ginger biscuits

MARTIN BENTON'S MENU
Baked salmon with cucumber and a lemon cream sauce, New Welsh broth, Cinnamon
puddings with cider sauce and apples

PETER SAYERS'S MENU
Avocado pear with a redcurrant dressing, Monkfish in a blanket, Upside-down apple
pecan pie

*1 small whole hot-smoked freshwater
eel or 8 oz (225 g) fillets
Thinly pared rind of ½ lime, cut into
thin strips*

FOR THE PANCAKES
*1 10 oz (275 g) non-floury potato
(preferably Romano or Désirée)
1 well-flavoured eating apple
2 teaspoons barley flour, sifted
1 generous tablespoon thick soured
cream
1 egg yolk
1 teaspoon honey
½ teaspoon grated fresh or good-
quality bottled horseradish
Salt and pepper
A little butter or bacon fat*

FOR THE SALAD
*2 leaves Lollo Rosso lettuce, torn
4–8 small tender leaves French or wild
sorrel, shredded
4 radishes (preferably French
Breakfast variety), finely sliced
A few fronds of fresh dill
A few snipped and whole thin fresh
chives
2 rashers smoked streaky bacon, rind
removed
2 teaspoons fresh lime juice
Sea salt and freshly ground white or
black pepper
4 chive flowers, to decorate (optional)*

If using a whole eel, remove the skin in one piece if possible, otherwise slice the eel into manageable lengths before skinning. Fillet in 2 in (5 cm) long slices and carefully replace in the skin for later heating. Blanch the strips of lime rind in boiling water until tender. Drain and reserve.

For the pancakes, peel the potato and apple, then grate on a medium fine grater or food processor disc. Place in a clean tea towel and wring out the excess moisture by firmly twisting the ends of the towel. Put the drained potato and apple in a bowl and mix in the sifted barley flour, soured cream, egg yolk, honey and seasonings. Heat a cast iron blini pan or griddle over a gentle heat until thoroughly hot and brush with a little butter or bacon fat. Roughly pile the mixture into the indentations (or use muffin rings on a griddle pan) and press down a little. Cook gently for 5–10 minutes, or until the undersides are golden brown. Turn with a palette knife and cook on the other sides until these too are golden brown and the potato in the centre is cooked through. Press down a little from time to time. When cooked, remove the pan from the heat but keep the pancakes warm in the pan until ready to serve.

To make the salad, mix together all the ingredients except the bacon, lime juice, seasonings and chive flowers. For the dressing, dice the bacon finely and fry until crisp. Shortly before serving the salad, add the lime juice to the hot bacon fat and immediately pour over the salad leaves.

To assemble the dish, heat the eel in its skin (wrapped in foil, if you wish) in a medium hot oven, at gas mark 6, 400°F (200°C), for 5–10 minutes. Alternatively, heat under a medium hot grill, as far from the source of heat as possible. Remove the eel from its wrapping and serve the hot fillets on hot pancakes with the slightly warm salad, decorated with the chive flowers (if using).

Scalloped beef platter

I adapted this from the old English tradition of serving beef with oysters – an excellent combination, though no longer the cheap dish it was. You could easily just toss the meat, scallops and mushrooms together with the pasta for a quick, if rather extravagant, pasta dish and serve with a simple salad.

Dried bitter orange peel is available from Scandinavian and German suppliers. Alternatively you could peel, dry and grate your own when Seville oranges are in season. Use organically grown fruit for preference.

It is possible to buy porcini-flavoured oil but it is much more satisfying to make your own by soaking a small quantity of good-quality dried mushrooms in very good-quality olive oil, protected from the light, for at least 1 year, and preferably 2. The results are worth the wait.

8 oz (225 g) trimmed fillet of beef (marbled with fat and well hung)
10 fl oz (300 ml) good unsalted beef stock
5 fl oz (150 ml) concentrated seasoned beef stock
1 tablespoon balsamic vinegar or good-quality wine vinegar
8 oz (225 g) trimmed rump steak
1 scant teaspoon tarragon mustard
1 teaspoon crème fraîche or Greek yoghurt
½ teaspoon powdered dried ceps (porcini)
¼ teaspoon powdered dried bitter orange peel
Salt and black pepper
Cep oil or olive oil, to brush
4 fresh king scallops or 6–8 smaller scallops
2 tablespoons beef dripping
Fresh or dried bitter orange peel, to garnish (optional)

Chill the fillet well (or quickly half-freeze it) before slicing into thin rounds (you should manage at least 16). Bring the unsalted beef stock to the boil, then reduce to a bare simmer. Warm the concentrated beef stock until hand hot, then add the balsamic or wine vinegar. Poach the slices of fillet very gently in the unsalted beef stock (this may need to be done in 3 batches) until just starting to lose their pinkness. Transfer immediately to the warm concentrated stock until ready to serve.

Now chop the rump steak. When roughly chopped, spread the mixture thinly on the chopping board and sprinkle on the mustard, crème fraîche or yoghurt and seasonings. These will blend in as you continue to chop very finely. Form the mixture into marble-sized balls (again, aim for about 16, perhaps with a spare to test for seasoning and doneness). Pre-heat a grill and grill-pan until very hot, brush or toss the meat balls with cep oil or olive oil and grill as quickly as possible in order to caramelise the outside but keep the inside rare. Remove to a warm platter and cover with foil.

Shortly before serving, clean and trim the scallops, washing briskly, and reserving the corals for another recipe (or if mixing all the ingredients into pasta, blanch and fry quickly with the rounds at the last minute). Slice each king scallop into 4 rounds (if using smaller scallops, slice each one into 2 rounds) and place on kitchen paper to absorb excess moisture. Meanwhile, heat the dripping in a small frying pan or shallow saucepan until smoking hot. Slide the scallops into the hot dripping (they may need to be done in 2 batches) and toss and shake the pan for just over 1 minute. The out-side of the scallops should be tinged with brown but they should remain soft and springy to the touch. Drain quickly, sprinkle with a little bitter orange peel if you wish and serve with the sliced fillet and meat patties.

Pasta with cep and oyster mushroom sauce

1 small packet dried ceps (porcini), weighing about 1 oz (25 g)
2 tablespoons Madeira, warmed
4–6 oz (100–175 g) fresh oyster mushrooms
½ oz (15 g) unsalted butter
1 teaspoon Dijon mustard
2 small cloves baked garlic (see note on p. 54)
Salt and pepper
5 tablespoons good beef stock
1 tablespoon thick crème fraîche or Greek yoghurt
A pinch of pounded saffron strands (optional)
6 oz (175 g) dried thin-cut pasta ribbons or 6–8 oz (175–225 g) fresh taglierini, preferably green and white (paglia e fieno)
Chopped carrot tops or fresh flat leaf parsley, to garnish

Soak the dried mushrooms in the warmed Madeira for about 1 hour. Drain and slice, reserving the soaking liquid. This should be strained through a double thickness of muslin.

Now slice the oyster mushrooms roughly and place in a heavy-based or non-stick pan with the butter, mus-tard, garlic and a little salt and pepper. Cover and cook over a gentle heat for a few minutes until the mushrooms yield their liquid. Remove the lid, increase the heat and drive off the excess liquid. Then pour the Madeira (previously used to soak the ceps) into the pan and reduce until evaporated. Add the beef stock and reduce until syrupy. Lower the heat a little and stir in the crème fraîche or yoghurt, along with the saffron, if using. Stir well and correct the seasoning.

Cook the pasta, according to the instructions on the packet, in fairly salty boiling water, until *al dente* (cook fresh pasta for only a couple of minutes). Drain well, then toss into the mushroom sauce.

To serve, pile the sauced pasta in the centre of the individual plates and sprinkle with the chopped carrot tops or flat leaf parsley.

Young carrots and fennel

1 bunch young carrots
5 fl oz (150 ml) good beef stock
Juice and finely grated rind of ½ small orange
1 teaspoon honey
1½ oz (40 g) unsalted butter
A pinch of salt
½ teaspoon crushed, toasted coriander seeds or ¼ teaspoon ground coriander
Freshly ground black pepper
8 baby fennel bulbs or 1–2 large bulbs, cut into wedges
1 teaspoon Pernod or Anise

Wash and trim the carrots and place them whole in a single layer in a large saucepan. Add the stock, orange juice and rind, honey, ½ oz (15 g) butter

and the salt, cover tightly and cook gently until almost tender but still crisp. At this stage, remove the lid, increase the heat, and quickly reduce the liquid to a coating syrup. Keep tossing the carrots until coated in syrup. Sprinkle with coriander, and freshly ground black pepper to taste.

Now trim the fennel, discarding the base and stems but retaining the fronds. Parboil in rapidly boiling salted water until tender but still crisp. Drain well and place in a baking dish with 1 oz (25 g) butter and the Pernod or Anise. Season with salt and pepper. Bake in a low oven (or cook in a heavy-based pan over the gentlest hob-heat) until perfectly tender, but not limp.

Finely chop the reserved fennel fronds, sprinkle over the baked fennel and serve the vegetables on individual plates or on a separate platter.

Kent strawberry kissel with scented geranium meringue

To make the geranium sugar, grind one dozen freshly picked medium-sized geranium leaves of any scented, edible variety with 6 oz (175 g) caster sugar (preferably the light, raw type) in a coffee-grinder. Spread out on baking sheets and dry gently in a low oven, at gas mark ½, 250°F (120°C), for 10–15 minutes, until no longer moist. Store in a jar with a tight-fitting lid until needed.

'Instant ruin.'
SIR ROY STRONG

FOR THE KISSEL
1 lb (450 g) Kent strawberries
2 tablespoons fruit sugar
Lemon juice
1 teaspoon arrowroot

FOR THE MERINGUE
3 egg whites
A pinch of cream of tartar or salt (optional)
6 oz (175 g) geranium sugar (see above)
1 teaspoon lime or lemon juice
1 teaspoon cornflour
5 fl oz (150 ml) clotted cream
2-3 oz (50-75 g) Alpine strawberries, to decorate
4-6 tiny geranium leaves, to decorate

To make the kissel, dry and hull the strawberries and divide into 2 equal batches. Sprinkle the first batch with 1 tablespoon fruit sugar and a squeeze of lemon juice. Set aside for 1–2 hours until the juices begin to seep. Place the second batch in a stainless steel saucepan with 1 tablespoon fruit sugar and a squeeze of lemon juice, and cook gently until completely tender. Purée (no need to sieve) and return to the saucepan. Blend the arrowroot with a little cold water, or some juice from the first batch of strawberries, then stir into the purée and bring back to the boil, stirring constantly. Once thickened, cook very gently for another couple of minutes. Then allow to cool completely. Now purée the first batch of strawberries, along with any syrup produced, and blend with the cooked purée. Check for sweetness, adding a little fruit sugar or lemon juice as needed, then chill until ready to serve.

For the meringues, whisk the egg whites until very stiff (a pinch of cream of tartar or salt helps). Then whisk in half the geranium sugar, whisking until completely stiff. If using a food mixer, the remaining sugar can also be whisked in at high speed. Otherwise fold in gently, along with the citrus juice and cornflour. Pile on to a greaseproof paper-lined baking sheet and shape into 4 or 6 nests. Bake in a moderate oven, at gas mark 3, 325°F (160°C), for about 40 minutes, until lightly tinged with brown and surface-dry. Remove from the oven and ease off the baking sheet. Fill each nest with a little clotted cream, and decorate with the Alpine strawberries. Place a geranium leaf at one edge of each meringue, and serve with a jugful of kissel.

THE SEMI-FINAL

Round One

ALISON RIDDELL'S MENU

·

STARTER

Marinade of salmon rillettes with brown bread and butter

·

MAIN COURSE

Springtime chicken with grapes, wine and elderflower
Minted Jersey Royals
Green salad

·

DESSERT

Spiced amber cups with orange bouchées

Marinade of salmon rillettes

8 oz (225 g) salmon fillet, very finely sliced
Juice of 1 lime
2 rounded teaspoons coriander seeds, crushed
2 teaspoons chopped fresh parsley
2 spring onions, finely sliced
Salt and freshly ground black pepper
Cucumber slices, to garnish
4 teaspoons Greek yoghurt, to garnish
4 thin wedges of lime, to garnish

Mix all the ingredients (except those for the garnish) gently together, cover and chill for 1 hour or more. Serve surrounded by cucumber slices and topped with the Greek yoghurt, a thin wedge of lime and a sprinkling of freshly ground black pepper. Accompany with slices of brown bread and butter.

Springtime chicken with grapes, wine and elderflower

---

4 chicken breasts, skinned
1 lb (450 g) seedless green grapes, crushed
10 fl oz (300 ml) dry white wine
4 large cloves garlic, halved
4–5 elderflower heads (creamy and not too open)
5–6 sprigs fresh marjoram or oregano
Salt and pepper
5–6 fl oz (150–175 ml) chicken stock
2 egg yolks, beaten
1 scant teaspoon cornflour, slaked with a little water
8 seedless green grapes, halved, to garnish
4 sprigs of fresh marjoram, to garnish (optional)
4 fresh vine leaves, to garnish

Place the chicken, grapes, wine and garlic in a heavy-based pan or casserole, cover and set aside in a cool place for 1 hour or more.

Now add the elderflower heads to the pan, together with the herbs and salt and pepper, bring to a very gentle simmer and poach for about 20 minutes. When the chicken is cooked, ladle out about 10 fl oz (300 ml) of the poaching liquid into a smaller pan and add a little chicken stock, being careful not to drown the delicate elderflower flavour. Taste and adjust the seasoning as necessary. Then whisk in the beaten egg yolks and the slaked cornflour, and stir continuously over a low heat till the sauce just thickens.

Serve each chicken breast coated in a little sauce and garnished with grape halves, a sprig of marjoram, if using, and a fresh vine leaf.

Minted Jersey Royals

1½ lb (750 g) Jersey Royal potatoes (all about the same size)
2 tablespoons fresh mint leaves
1 oz (25 g) unsalted butter
Salt and pepper
3 fl oz (85 ml) chicken stock or water

Scrub the potatoes and place them in a pan on a bed of mint, with the butter, salt and pepper and the stock or water. Cover with a tight-fitting lid and cook very gently for 30–35 minutes. Serve with a crisp green salad on side plates.

Spiced amber cups with orange bouchées

'If grown-ups eat jelly, this is what they eat. Very gentle, very warm, very lasting. I must have the recipe. It's absolutely delicious.'

RAYMOND BLANC

FOR THE AMBER CUPS
2 teaspoons gelatine
5 fl oz (150 ml) orange juice (some of which should be from blood oranges)
8 fl oz (250 ml) Moscatel de Valencia
4–5 fresh young rosemary sprigs, crushed in a mortar and pestle
A generous grating of nutmeg
Finely grated rind of ½ orange
2 tablespoons whipped cream
½ teaspoon caster sugar
A dash of almond liqueur or almond essence

FOR THE ORANGE BOUCHÉES
1 egg
1½ oz (40 g) soft margarine
2 oz (50 g) caster sugar (preferably golden)
½ teaspoon finely grated orange rind
1 oz (25 g) ground almonds
1 oz (25 g) self-raising flour

For the amber cups, melt the gelatine in the orange juice. When completely dissolved, add the mixture to the wine, together with the rosemary and the nutmeg. Check the flavouring and strain through muslin. Add a little grated orange and fill 4 small glasses about two-thirds full. Refrigerate for 2 hours. Before serving, mix the whipped cream with the caster sugar and almond liqueur (or essence), and top each glass with a teaspoonful of sweetened cream.

To make the orange bouchées, whisk together the egg, margarine and caster sugar. Add the grated orange rind and the ground almonds and fold in the flour. Bake at gas mark 6, 400°F (200°C), for about 8 minutes in very well-oiled mini bun tins. Serve with the amber cups.

PETER SAYERS'S MENU

·
STARTER
Prawn custard
·
MAIN COURSE
Lamb chops with a mushroom
stuffing, wrapped in filo pastry
Chive sauce
A selection of vegetables
·
DESSERT
Hazelnut meringue gateau with
raspberry coulis

Prawn custard

8 oz (225 g) cooked shelled prawns
(save a few prawns with shells for
decoration)
3–4 spring onions
3 size 3 eggs
1 teaspoon grated fresh ginger
8 fl oz (250 ml) chicken or fish stock
3 tablespoons dry sherry (optional)
Salt and pepper

Chop the prawns and spring onions
finely. In a bowl beat the eggs and
add the prawns, spring onions, grated
ginger, stock and sherry if using. Season with salt and pepper. Mix well
and pour into 4 buttered or oiled
ramekins or 1 larger dish. Place in
a shallow baking tray containing
enough hot water to come halfway up
the sides of the ramekins or dish.

Cook for 25–35 minutes at gas mark
3, 325°F (160°C), until the custard is
just set in the centre.

Lamb chops with a mushroom stuffing, wrapped in filo pastry

1 small onion
2 oz (50 g) button mushrooms
3 oz (75 g) butter
4 tablespoons olive oil
1 oz (25 g) fresh breadcrumbs
1 tablespoon chopped fresh parsley or 2
teaspoons dried parsley
1 size 3 egg, beaten
Salt and pepper
8 lamb loin chops
8 sheets filo pastry

Finely chop the onion and mushrooms. Heat ½ oz (15 g) butter with 1
tablespoon olive oil until bubbling.
Add the onion and mushrooms and
cook until the butter and oil have
been absorbed and the onions are
translucent. Remove from the heat
and allow to cool. Add the
breadcrumbs and parsley and enough
beaten egg to make a firm, moist
mixture. Season well with salt and
pepper.

Take the loin chops and remove
approximately 2 in (5 cm) meat from
the end of the rib bone, leaving the
bone bare. Season both sides of each
chop with salt and pepper. In a frying

pan heat 1 oz (25 g) butter and the remaining 3 tablespoons olive oil until bubbling. Quickly seal both sides of each chop, 2 or 3 at a time. Now divide the mushroom mixture between the 8 chops, placing the stuffing on the meaty part of one side.

Divide each sheet of filo pastry into 6 in (15 cm) squares, allowing 2–3 squares per chop. Cover the filo pastry with a damp cloth when not working with it, to prevent it drying out. Melt the remaining 1½ oz (40 g) butter. Lay out a square of filo pastry and brush with butter. Fold one corner to the centre and brush this with butter. Lay a chop on the pastry with the rib bone lying over the folded section. Wrap the remaining pastry round the chop, and repeat with another 1–2 squares depending upon their thickness. The bone will stick out of the parcel but make sure there is a reasonable seal around it. Repeat this process with all the chops.

Place the parcels in a baking dish and cook at gas mark 6, 400°F (200°C), for 20–35 minutes, depending on whether you prefer the meat pink or well done. If the pastry looks too brown, cover with foil and reduce the heat.

Chive sauce

2 oz (50 g) shallots, finely chopped
4 fl oz (120 ml) dry white wine
2 fl oz (50 ml) chicken stock
10 fl oz (300 ml) whipping cream
1 tablespoon spinach purée
2 tablespoons chopped fresh chives
1 tablespoon lemon juice
Salt and pepper
3 oz (75 g) butter

Add the chopped shallots to the wine in a small saucepan. Bring to simmering point and reduce, uncovered, until there is approximately 1 tablespoon moist purée left. Boil the chicken stock with 1 fl oz (25 ml) water and the whipping cream until it has reduced by approximately one-third. Blend or process the spinach purée, chives, 3 tablespoons cold water and the shallot reduction. Add the stock and cream, and the lemon juice. Season with salt and pepper and blend again for 30 seconds. Return to a saucepan, reheat but do not boil, and whisk in the butter, a small piece at a time. Keep warm in a bowl over warm water until required. Serve with the lamb parcels and a selection of fresh vegetables.

Hazelnut meringue gateau with raspberry coulis

4 size 3 egg whites
8 oz (225 g) caster sugar
A few drops of vanilla essence
½ teaspoon vinegar
5 oz (150 g) hazelnuts, roasted and ground
10 fl oz (300 ml) double cream
4 oz (100 g) granulated sugar
2 teaspoons liquid glucose
10 oz (275 g) fresh or frozen raspberries, thawed if frozen
Juice of ½ lemon
Icing sugar, to decorate

Whisk the egg whites until stiff but not dry. Add the caster sugar, 1 tablespoon at a time, and continue whisking until the mixture stands in peaks. Whisk in a few drops of vanilla essence and the vinegar, then fold in the ground hazelnuts. Divide the mixture between 2 buttered, floured and lined 8 in (20 cm) sandwich cake tins, and level the tops with a knife. Bake for 30–40 minutes at gas mark 5, 375° F (190° C), until the cakes are crisp on top. Allow to cool.

Whisk the cream until just stiff and sweeten to taste. Refrigerate until required. Now put the granulated sugar and glucose in a small saucepan with 4½ fl oz (135 ml) water, and boil for approximately 10 minutes. If crystals form, brush the inside of the pan with cold water. Set aside to cool. Then combine the syrup with the raspberries and lemon juice and blend or process until smooth. Sieve, and keep in the refrigerator until required.

To assemble the gateau, place one cake on a serving plate, spread over the cream, place the second cake on top and dust with icing sugar. Serve with the raspberry coulis.

BRIAN GLOVER'S MENU

WINNER

·
STARTER
Salad of smoked trout and samphire with a tomato vinaigrette
·
MAIN COURSE
Guineafowl marinated in basil and olive oil
Red pepper relish
Turnip gratin
Mixture of spring vegetables
·
DESSERT
Cardamom cake with papaya and rhubarb

Salad of smoked trout and samphire with a tomato vinaigrette

When samphire is out of season, an alternative is thin asparagus, to which you could add very fine green beans to bring down the cost. Use hot-smoked trout, not the translucent type that looks like smoked salmon.

5 tablespoons olive oil
1 tablespoon lemon juice
2 tablespoons chopped fresh dill
1 tablespoon chopped fresh chives
A little sugar
Salt and pepper
2 salad tomatoes, skinned, de-seeded and finely diced
8 oz (225 g) samphire, washed and picked over
8 oz (225 g) smoked trout, skinned and flaked
1 large bunch mixed salad leaves (watercress, lettuce, rocket, sorrel, etc.)
8 cherry tomatoes, halved, to garnish

Make the dressing with the olive oil, lemon juice, dill and chives. Season to taste with sugar, salt and pepper, then add the finely diced tomatoes. Lightly steam the samphire, making sure it stays crisp. Dress with two-thirds of the dressing while still warm. Allow to cool, then mix in the smoked trout. Use the remaining dressing to toss the salad leaves. Arrange the salad and samphire on individual plates and decorate with the cherry tomatoes. Serve with granary rolls or bread and unsalted butter.

Guineafowl marinated in basil and olive oil

I think it's a lovely idea to marinate in flavoured oils, and this is a gentle marinade. You must use a really good guineafowl, ideally free-range, corn-fed.

*Breasts and legs of 4 guineafowl (use
rest of birds to make stock or soup and
use flesh in a salad)
1 large bunch of fresh basil
1 large onion, roughly chopped
5 fl oz (150 ml) olive oil
1 clove garlic, chopped
6 sprigs of fresh thyme
2 shallots, chopped
2 carrots, chopped
6–8 fl oz (175–250 ml) red wine
Salt
1 bayleaf
2 fl oz (50 ml) port
½ oz (15 g) butter*

Skin the guineafowl breasts and slash the legs in 2 or 3 places. Place in a non-metallic dish in a single layer. Process or blend the basil (reserving a few leaves for garnish), onion, olive oil, garlic and 2 sprigs thyme. Pour the mixture over the guineafowl and rub in well. Refrigerate for 24 hours, turning once.

The next day, dry off the legs, brown them in a non-stick pan, and place in a casserole. Brown the shallots and carrots in the same pan, then deglaze with a little red wine. Add to the casserole. Season the legs with salt, then pour over the remaining wine. Add the bayleaf and tuck in 4 sprigs fresh thyme. Cover and cook for 30–40 minutes at gas mark 6, 400°F (200°C).

Dry off the breasts and brown quickly on both sides in a non-stick pan. Transfer to a baking tray, season with salt and cook at gas mark 6–7, 400–425°F (200–220°C), for 10 minutes. Allow to rest for 10 minutes, covered with foil.

Remove the legs from the casserole and keep warm with the breasts. Strain the juices into a small pan. Skim off any fat, taste and adjust the seasoning. Bring the juices to the boil and add the port. Reduce until syrupy. Swirl in the butter at the end, to add gloss to the sauce. Garnish with a few basil leaves and serve.

Red pepper relish

This recipe has grown out of a liking for grilled peppers. 'Brian never uses a red pepper unless he grills it first,' is a popular cry among my friends. The smoky flavour goes well with the guineafowl and it is also good with rabbit.

2 small red onions, finely chopped
2–3 tablespoons olive oil
1 clove garlic, crushed
2 large red peppers, grilled, skinned, de-seeded and diced
2 sprigs of fresh thyme, chopped
Balsamic or wine vinegar
1 bunch of fresh basil, torn into small pieces
Salt and black pepper

Fry the onions in the olive oil until soft but not coloured. Add the garlic and fry for 2 more minutes. Now add the red peppers and thyme, and cook over a gentle heat for 10–15 minutes. Raise the heat and add vinegar to taste. Stir in the basil towards the end. Season to taste with salt and black pepper.

Turnip gratin

I served the guineafowl with this Turnip gratin as well as the Red pepper relish and a mixture of fresh peas, broad beans, French beans and asparagus tips, all lightly cooked and tossed in a little butter. Raymond Blanc said the green vegetables were unnecessary and I'm sure he's right.

1½ lb (750 g) young summer turnips, peeled
1 oz (25 g) butter
Salt and pepper
1 clove garlic, halved
8 fl oz (250 ml) double cream
A few sprigs of fresh thyme, to garnish

Grate the turnips fairly coarsely. Fry in the butter over a medium heat until just soft and beginning to brown. Season to taste with salt and pepper. Lightly rub individual gratin dishes (or one large gratin dish) with garlic and butter. Put the grated turnip in the dish or dishes. Pour over the cream and cook at gas mark 6–7, 400–425°F (200–220°C), for 15–20 minutes until nicely browned. Garnish with a few sprigs of thyme and serve.

Cardamom cake with papaya and rhubarb

I love cardamom in sweet things and I notice that Jocelyn Dimbleby uses it a lot too. This cake is one of my standbys – it's very moist and light, in fact more like a pudding than a cake.

'A tropical ending. Carmen Miranda Pudding.'
LOYD GROSSMAN
'Delicious.'
RAYMOND BLANC

FOR THE CAKE
4 oz (100 g) butter
3 oz (75 g) caster sugar
2 eggs, beaten
2 oz (50 g) ground almonds
4 oz (100 g) self-raising flour, sifted
1 teaspoon ground cardamom
Grated rind and juice of 1 lime
Icing sugar, to decorate

FOR THE SYRUP
2 oz (50 g) granulated sugar
3 strips lime rind
4 cardamom pods, crushed
Juice of 1 lime

FOR THE FRUIT
1 papaya
Lime juice
1 lb (450 g) rhubarb
2 oz (50 g) caster sugar
5 fl oz (150 ml) double cream, whipped

To make the cake, first cream the butter and sugar. Beat in the eggs, a little at a time, then fold in the ground almonds, sifted flour, cardamom and lime rind and juice. Turn into a 7 in (18 cm) lined and buttered cake tin and bake at gas mark 4, 350°F (180°C), for 30–40 minutes until risen and firm to the touch.

Meanwhile, make the syrup. Dissolve the sugar in 5 fl oz (150 ml) water, and add the lime rind and cardamom. Boil for 3 minutes, then leave to infuse until the cake is ready. When the cake is done, turn it out and, while it is still warm, prick it all over the top with a skewer. Reheat the syrup to just under boiling point, add the lime juice and strain over the warm cake. Leave to cool.

Peel, de-seed and slice the papaya. Arrange on a plate and sprinkle with the lime juice. Leave for at least 1 hour. Cut the rhubarb into chunks and place in a pan with the caster sugar. Add 6 fl oz (175 ml) water and poach gently so that the rhubarb stays whole. Remove the rhubarb with a slotted spoon, reserving the syrup. Keep half the rhubarb aside for decoration. Roughly purée the remainder and fold into the whipped cream. Sweeten with the poaching syrup.

To assemble the pudding, sprinkle the top of the cake thickly with sifted icing sugar and make caramelised lines across the top with a heated skewer. Serve each slice of cake with papaya and rhubarb on one side and some rhubarb cream on the other.

Round Two

MARTIN BENTON'S MENU

——————

Sprue soup with mushrooms and garlic croûtons

·

MAIN COURSE

Fillet of pork in a red wine sauce with chicory
New potatoes

·

DESSERT

Oranges and strawberries with an orange cream

Sprue soup with mushrooms and garlic croûtons

——————

This is based on an idea of Freddy Girardet's, although he uses even more cream. Sprue grass is the traditional English asparagus and I feel it's better than the ordinary stuff. If you use asparagus rather than sprue then you must peel and trim it to get rid of the woody bits.

——————

20 sprue or thin asparagus spears
3 shallots
3 oz (75 g) unsalted butter
8 fl oz (250 ml) whipping cream
Salt and white pepper
1 slice stale white bread
1 clove garlic
1 teaspoon olive oil
4 mushroom caps
2 teaspoons chopped fresh parsley

——————

Trim the woody base from the sprue or asparagus, if necessary, throw into a pan of lightly salted boiling water and simmer for about 5 minutes until tender. Drain and reserve the cooking liquor. Cut off the 8 thickest sprue tips, halve lengthways and reserve. Coarsely chop the remaining sprue, then chop 2 shallots. Cook the shallots in a saucepan with 1 oz (25 g) butter until soft. Then add the chopped sprue and 8 fl oz (250 ml) of the reserved liquor. Bring to the boil, add the cream and reduce for a few minutes. Blend or process the mixture with 1 oz (25 g) butter, strain into a clean saucepan and season with salt and white pepper.

Cut the bread into ¼ in (5 mm) cubes and toast in a hot oven at gas mark 6, 200°F (400°C), until crisp and brown. Chop the garlic and remaining shallot together and set aside. Heat the oil until very hot in a small frying pan, sear the mushrooms until they just start to give out their juices, remove and keep warm. Turn the heat down and add 1 oz (25 g) butter to the pan. Fry the chopped garlic and shallot, then add the toasted croûtons and mix.

To serve, reheat the soup and heat the sprue tips in a little cooking liquor. Ladle the soup into 4 bowls and place a mushroom cap, top down, in the centre of each. Fill each cap with the croûton mixture, sprinkle with a little parsley and garnish with the sprue tips.

Fillet of pork in a red wine sauce with chicory

I believe pork tenderloin is underrated and I think this dish really works well. If you can't get hold of chicory then leeks would make a good alternative. Don't serve any other vegetables with this dish, just boiled potatoes, ideally new ones, tossed in butter.

1½ lb (750 g) pork fillet
A few fresh sage leaves
Black pepper
2 fl oz (50 ml) olive oil
18 fl oz (520 ml) red wine
½ onion
1 small courgette
½ leek
¼ fennel bulb
1 clove garlic
A sprig of fresh tarragon
A sprig of fresh parsley
4½ oz (120 g) unsalted butter
2 shallots
1½ tablespoons sugar
4 heads chicory
Juice of 1 lemon
Salt
1 teaspoon Dijon mustard

Slice the pork fillet diagonally into ¾ in (2 cm) thick 'nuggets', then shred some of the sage leaves, reserving the rest for garnishing. Season the pork pieces with black pepper and the sage. Mix the olive oil and 4 fl oz (120 ml) red wine in a ceramic dish. Add the pork and leave to marinate.

Meanwhile, chop the onion, cour-gette, leek, fennel, garlic and herbs for the stock. Sweat the vegetables in 1 oz (25 g) butter, then add 10 fl oz (300 ml) water and simmer for 5 min-utes. Add the herbs and simmer for 5 more minutes. Strain and reserve the liquor. Dice 1½ oz (40 g) butter and chill. Chop the shallots and sweat in 1 oz (25 g) butter. Add the stock, 14 fl oz (400 ml) wine and 2 tea-spoons sugar. Reduce and set aside. Wipe the chicory and cut into pieces, discarding the hard core at the base. Combine in a bowl with 1 teaspoon sugar and the lemon juice. Grill the pork pieces without further oil, cover and keep warm. Melt 1 oz (25 g) butter in a large heavy-based pan. Add the chicory and fry briefly, making sure that it remains crisp. Season with salt, pepper and sugar.

To serve, arrange a bed of chicory on each plate and place the pork pieces on top, garnished with some sage leaves. Reheat the wine reduc-tion, beat in the mustard, season with salt and black pepper, and whisk in the chilled butter. Strain and pour around the pork and chicory.

Oranges and strawberries with an orange cream

The oranges must be knife-segmented – they mustn't have any skin or pith on them. When you're making the syrup to poach the oranges and you've added the orange juice to the caramel, take heart. It looks like it will all go horribly wrong but it boils down eventually. I was horrified when I first did it. The orange cream is a doddle. Don't try and use yoghurt instead of cream – there's no substitute for the real thing. It sounds wicked, but if you're going to treat yourself, then the heck with it!

'A very classical sweet.'
ANTON EDELMANN

FOR THE FRUIT
6 oranges
4 passion fruit
4 oz (100 g) caster sugar
1 fl oz (25 ml) Grand Marnier
10 strawberries

FOR THE CREAM
2 egg yolks
1½ oz (40 g) caster sugar
½ (15 g) plain white flour
6 fl oz (175 ml) milk
½ vanilla pod, split
1 oz (25 g) orange jelly marmalade
5 fl oz (150 ml) double cream
1 teaspoon Grand Marnier
4 small fresh mint leaves, to decorate

Thinly peel the rind from 3 of the oranges and slice into fine strips. Blanch in boiling water for a minute and drain. Knife-segment all the oranges, catching and reserving the juice. Cut open the passion fruit and reserve the juice. Melt the caster sugar in a saucepan until just brown. Add the orange juice and reduce to a light syrup. Now add the blanched rind, Grand Marnier and passion fruit juice. Bring to the boil and stir in the orange segments. Remove from the heat and leave to cool. Halve the strawberries, add them to the cool oranges, mix carefully and refrigerate.

For the orange cream, first make the pastry cream by whisking the egg yolks in a bowl with about ½ oz (15 g) sugar until the mixture is thick. Mix in the flour. Now put the milk, remaining sugar and the vanilla pod together in a pan. Bring to the boil, then remove the vanilla pod. Whisk a little boiling milk into the egg yolk mixture. Add this to the milk in the pan and bring to the boil, stirring. Simmer for a few minutes, then remove from the heat and allow to cool.

Now whisk together 2 oz (50 g) pastry cream with the orange jelly marmalade, 2½ fl oz (65 ml) syrup from the oranges, 2½ fl oz (65 ml) double cream and the Grand Marnier. (Cover and refrigerate the remaining pastry cream and use for another dessert.) Lightly whisk the remaining double cream and fold into the orange cream mixture.

To serve, arrange a star of orange and strawberry pieces around 4 heatproof plates, then put a little orange cream in the centre of each plate. Place under a very hot grill to warm the fruit and lightly brown the cream. Decorate each plate with a small mint leaf.

51

SILVIJA DAVIDSON'S MENU

•
STARTER
Crabmeat filo tarts
•
MAIN COURSE
Gloucester pork roll with herb
garden stuffing
Golden risotto
Butter-tossed garden peas and
cucumber
•
DESSERT
Soft cheese dumplings with a
fresh apricot sauce

Crabmeat filo tarts

Freshly caught crab is essential and
it tastes much better if you cook it
yourself. Frozen broad beans are
excellent for this dish and they
don't even need cooking: simply
take them out of their jackets.
(Only 4 oz (100 g) will be needed.)
Dulse may be bought, in small or
large quantities, from good
wholefood shops.

*'This recipe could persuade me to eat
filo pastry.'*
ANTON EDELMANN

1 × 2 lb (1 kg) freshly cooked crab or
1 × 7 oz (200 g) pack fresh crab
meat, white and brown separate
4 sheets filo pastry
2 teaspoons ground coriander
1½ tablespoons melted unsalted butter
1 lb (450 g) young broad beans in
their pods
4 oz (100 g) small yellow pattypan
squashes or yellow courgettes
4 oz (100 g) fresh oyster mushrooms
1 teaspoon unsalted butter
1 teaspoon Dijon mustard
A pinch of salt
1 tablespoon dry rich sherry
(preferably Oloroso)
4 teaspoons crème fraîche
4 oz (100 g) Dunsyre Blue or 3 oz
(75 g) Roquefort cheese
½ teaspoon sherry vinegar, or
to taste
1 oz (25 g) fresh rye breadcrumbs
Sea salt
Freshly ground black pepper
½ oz (15 g) dried Scottish red dulse,
to garnish (optional)

If using a whole freshly cooked crab,
dismember it, extract the brown and
white meats and keep cool in separate
containers.

Fold each sheet of filo into 3 to
make a near-square shape and trim
one edge to produce a square. With a
small, sharp knife, cut through any
folds to give 3 squares of pastry per
sheet. Using a pastry brush, blend the
ground coriander into the melted
butter. Brush one side of a filo square
with butter, and press gently into a

Yorkshire pudding tin. Brush a second square with the butter and press on top of the piece in the tin at an angle of 30°, so that once the third sheet is pressed into place, the edges of the tart shell look like flower petals. Repeat with the remaining squares of filo to produce 4 shells. Place a smaller tart tin, or scrunched-up foil, in each shell to prevent the centre from rising whilst cooking. Place the tins on a baking sheet and bake at gas mark 4, 350°F (180°C), for about 10 minutes, or until the pastry is brown-edged and crisp. When cooked, remove the smaller tins or foil from the centres, and ease the pastry shells out of their tins and into serving or warming dishes (large scallop shells look attractive).

Shell the broad beans (which should be as young and fresh as possible) and cook lightly in boiling salted water for 3–6 minutes until just tender. Drain, remove the jackets from the larger beans, and set aside. Slice the pattypan squashes into wedges, or the courgettes into rounds, and blanch in boiling, salted water for a couple of minutes. Drain and set aside.

Slice the oyster mushrooms quite finely and place in a heavy-based or non-stick frying pan with the butter, mustard and a small pinch of salt. Cover and cook over medium heat, shaking occasionally, until the juices are released. Remove the lid, increase the heat and pour in the sherry. Stir until evaporated, then add 3 teaspoons crème fraîche, stir through, and remove from the heat. Set aside.

Crumble one-third of the blue cheese into the container of brown crab meat, add 1 teaspoon crème fraîche, the sherry vinegar and breadcrumbs and season lightly to taste with sea salt and freshly ground black pepper. Divide this mixture between the 4 pastry cases. Gently mix together the white crab meat, broad beans, squashes or courgette and mushrooms and season to taste. Pile on top of the brown meat base and sprinkle with the remaining cheese.

Shortly before serving, place in a medium hot oven, at gas mark 4, 350°F (180°C), for 5–10 minutes, until the cheese has just melted, and serve warm. If using Scottish dulse as a garnish (it also adds interestingly to the range of textures and flavours), place the dried dulse in a cupful of tepid water for about 10 minutes and drain carefully before using as a 'bed' for the pastries. It may also be heated, but then it will crisp up – a different effect, though still interesting to eat.

Gloucester pork roll with herb garden stuffing

Slow cooking is important for this. Don't be tempted to cook it at a higher temperature to cut down the time it takes. And remember that resting time is as important as gentle roasting for final tenderness. All the pork I used in the *MasterChef* semi-final originated from the Gloucester Old Spot variety of pig, which has a heavier than usual fat covering, removed for this recipe.

In the absence of the specific herbs listed for the stuffing, use a little more of the liqueur, which certainly contains a good proportion of hyssop. Parsley may be used, of course, but lacks the strong aroma and pungency of the herbs mentioned.

I get my cold-smoked tenderloin from Heal Farm. You could use a cured pork loin, or *Lachsschinken* (from good delis), finely chopped and mixed into the herb stuffing, rather than in one piece.

To make oven-baked garlic: when roasting meat or poultry, place a whole unpeeled head of garlic, brushed with a little oil and wrapped in foil, in a medium hot oven for about 1 hour, or until soft and pulpy. Peel the cloves and squeeze the pulp into a small jar, cover with olive oil or vegetable oil and store in the refrigerator until needed. The cooked pulp is much easier to spread and mix than raw garlic, and also gives a more rounded flavour. But if you need to use the garlic raw, either rub the meat with a single clove, or crush one small clove with a little salt.

---

2 lb (1 kg) boned pork loin, rind and fat removed
Salt and pepper
1–2 oz (25–50 g) caul fat, in largish pieces
4 oz (100 g) thinly sliced streaky bacon, rinded

FOR THE STUFFING
1 bunch of watercress, trimmed
A sprig of fresh hyssop
1–2 leaves fresh lovage
2 leaves fresh bergamot
2 oz (50 g) fresh white breadcrumbs
2 teaspoons Elixir Végétal or Green Chartreuse
2 teaspoons pistachio or olive oil
1 oz (25 g) pistachio nuts, shelled
1 tablespoon marigold jelly or 1 teaspoon honey
1 small egg, beaten
4 oz (100 g) cured, cold-smoked tenderloin in one piece

FOR THE BASTE
1 tablespoon marigold jelly or honey
2 cloves oven-baked garlic
2 teaspoons wholegrain mustard
A splash of Madeira (optional)
A few sprigs of watercress, brushed with oil, to garnish (optional)

Season the inside of the joint lightly with salt and pepper. If the caul fat has been frozen or has a pronounced aroma, soak for 30 minutes in lightly vinegared tepid water before draining and drying carefully. Stretch the caul gently to form a net, trim any straggly pieces and set aside.

To make the stuffing, blanch the trimmed watercress by placing in a sieve and pouring over half a kettleful of boiling water. There's no need to refresh it, but squeeze out all excess moisture. The watercress, along with the herbs, can be chopped in a food processor with the breadcrumbs, or they can be chopped finely in the usual way. Mix with the liqueur, oil, nuts, jelly or honey and beaten egg.

If using the tenderloin in one piece, cut a slit in the eye of the loin muscle, all the way along the joint, and wedge the tenderloin into it. Pack the stuffing around the tenderloin, then roll the loin-flap gently but firmly around the stuffing.

For the baste, mix together the jelly or honey, garlic and mustard and spread over the outside of the rolled-up joint. Stretch and flatten the bacon a little, then wrap round the joint in roughly interleaved fashion, using the strips of bacon to help keep the joint rolled up. Finally, drape a small piece of caul over each end of the joint, and a larger piece (or 2) around the whole joint. The caul will effectively cling to itself, but remove any further superfluous straggly pieces.

Place the joint, join-side down, in a suitable roasting dish and roast at gas mark 3, 325°F (160°C), for 1¼ hours. After the first hour, add a splash of Madeira, if you wish, and baste once or twice with the juices and Madeira. When cooked, the bacon and caul should be golden brown.

Rest for 30 minutes in a switched-off or slightly warm oven, lightly wrapped in a double thickness of foil. Slice (not too thinly) and serve with the roasting juices and accompaniments. Garnish with a few sprigs of watercress if you wish.

Golden risotto

It's worth paying the extra money for saffron rather than turmeric although the marigold petals also contribute to the flavour and colour. I grow my own pot marigolds which I then microwave dry between sheets of kitchen paper.

1 small shallot, peeled and finely diced
2 oz (50 g) unsalted butter
8 oz (225 g) rice (preferably Arborio)
1¾ pints (1 litre) strong vegetable or chicken stock
A good pinch of saffron strands, toasted and ground in a mortar and pestle with a pinch of sea salt
Finely grated rind of ½ lemon
12 leaves fresh lemon balm, roughly chopped
2 heads dried or 3–4 heads fresh marigold petals
2½ fl oz (65 ml) chilled sweet wine or juice of ½ lemon
Salt and pepper
Fresh marigold petals, to garnish (optional)

Soften the shallot in 1 oz (25 g) butter over a very gentle heat for about 5 minutes. Add the rice to the pan and stir to coat each grain with butter. After 2–3 minutes the grains will appear translucent. At this stage add a ladleful of very hot stock (keep the stock simmering alongside the risotto pan if possible), and stir gently until all the stock is absorbed. Add the saffron and another ladleful of stock, and stir occasionally until this is absorbed. Add the lemon rind, lemon balm and marigold petals, and keep gradually adding stock, stirring from time to time, until the rice is tender but retains a little bite (about 20 minutes from when the stock was first added). Keep the rice looking moist at all times.

When cooked as you wish, remove from the heat and stir in either the wine for a sweetish flavour, or the lemon juice for a sharper taste. The cold liquid will help stop further cooking. Taste and adjust the seasoning, then beat in the remaining 1 oz (25 g) butter, cover and allow to rest for a couple of minutes before serving, sprinkled with a few additional fresh marigold petals if you wish.

Butter-tossed garden peas and cucumber

For this recipe, cook fresh garden peas in their pods. They keep their colour and flavour and they're easy to pod afterwards.

1 lb (450 g) fresh young garden peas
in their pods
1 medium cucumber
2 tablespoons wine vinegar
2 teaspoons fruit sugar
A good pinch of salt
1 oz (25 g) unsalted butter
4 fresh borage leaves, finely sliced
A few borage flowers (optional)

Boil the peas in their pods, depending on size and freshness. Cool a little, then shell and set aside. Run the prongs of a fork firmly down the cucumber all the way round, in order to give a slightly serrated effect when cut. Halve lengthways, remove the seeds with a teaspoon and discard. Cut the cucumber into 3 in (7.5 cm) lengths, then either slice into ¼ in (5 mm) wide half-moon slices or into small chunks. Mix together the vinegar, sugar and salt and pour over the cucumber. Leave to marinate for at least 1 hour, preferably 3.

Shortly before serving, drain the cucumber well. Melt the butter in a large saucepan and toss the cucumber with the butter. Sauté until cooked to your liking, aiming to retain a little crispness. Add the shelled peas to the pan (with a little extra butter if all appears to have been absorbed). Stir and toss the vegetables for a further 2 minutes, then stir in the borage leaves and serve. If borage is flowering, a few blue flowers can be added to striking effect, visually and flavourwise.

Soft cheese dumplings with a fresh apricot sauce

This dish obviously reflects my Eastern European background. It's delicious hot and I find dried apricots are just as good as fresh ones. The best results are obtained from unpasteurised, whole-milk soft cheese. Avoid using skimmed milk fromage frais, as the flavour will be thinner and sharper (though the dumplings will still hold together if the cheese is well drained). Bitter almonds are imported from Scandinavia, but difficult to find. If you like a definite almond flavour, use just 1 drop true bitter almond essence, blended with the egg. When maple sugar is unavailable, use a little fine demerara (flavoured with a vanilla pod if possible) but do not allow to stand for long before serving.

'Fairly earth-moving.'
LOYD GROSSMAN

FOR THE DUMPLINGS
8 oz (225 g) firm or well-drained fromage frais
1 good tablespoon crème fraîche
2–3 tablespoons maple syrup, or to taste
2 teaspoons lemon juice
Finely grated rind of ½ lemon
2 teaspoons potato flour
1 oz (25 g) ground almonds, toasted
½ grated bitter almond (optional)
About 2 oz (50 g) fresh brioche crumbs or fresh white breadcrumbs
A pinch of salt
1 egg plus 1 egg yolk, beaten together
1 teaspoon vanilla essence
Toasted ground almonds, ground cinnamon and maple or fine demerara sugar, to roll dumplings

FOR THE SAUCE
5 fl oz (150 ml) Monbazillac or similar peachy dessert wine, plus a further 5 fl oz (150 ml) to marinate nectarines if necessary
2 tablespoons fruit sugar
1 fresh bayleaf
1 vanilla pod
Rind and juice of 1 lemon
14 oz (400 g) fresh apricots, halved and stoned
2 small nectarines

Mix all the dumpling ingredients together in the order given, except for those used to roll the cooked dumplings. The precise amount of crumbs needed will be determined by the water content of the cheese. Once mixed, chill for at least 30 minutes. If the mixture is too soft to shape, even after chilling, add a few more brioche crumbs or breadcrumbs until shaping is possible. Don't add any more potato flour, or the dumplings will be heavy. After chilling, lightly and roughly shape the mixture into marble-sized balls (at least 12, plus 1 or 2 for testing). Poach in barely simmering lightly salted water for about 15 minutes or until firm. The dumplings are not necessarily done as soon as they rise to the surface. Test by cutting one open. If not yet done, it will fall apart. When cooked, drain well on a folded tea towel or piece of kitchen paper and set aside to cool. (The dumplings may be made in advance and stored in the fridge for up to 24 hours.)

To make the sauce, simmer together the wine, fruit sugar and flavourings for 5 minutes. Then simmer the apricots gently in the syrup until tender. (If there is insufficient liquid to cover the apricots, add a little water, or some more wine.) Remove and drain the apricots, then purée them with a little of the strained syrup. (If the syrup seems watery, reduce it over a high heat before adding to the apricots.) Check the apricot purée for sweetness and add more syrup or fruit sugar as needed, or a further squeeze of lemon juice. If the consistency is too thick, add a little wine to the purée, then allow to cool. (The purée may also be made in advance and stored in the fridge for up to 24 hours.) Stone and slice the nectarines fairly thinly. If not very ripe, pour the hot reduced apricot poaching syrup over them and marinate for at least 1 hour. If sweet and ripe, marinate instead in 5 fl oz (150 ml) peachy wine.

Shortly before serving, toss the cool dumplings lightly in toasted ground almonds, then toss one-third in a plate of ground cinnamon, one-third in the maple or demerara sugar, and give the remainder a second coat of toasted almonds. Pour some sauce on to each plate and arrange one or more of each type of dumpling, and a quarter of the sliced drained nectarines, on top.

MARY HENDRY'S MENU

·

STARTER

Trout poached in Dry Martini
with a currant sauce, served with
frisée

·

MAIN COURSE

Fillet steak stuffed with
mushrooms and seasonings with a
wine sauce
Home-made parsleyed tagliatelle
Carrot salad

·

DESSERT

Meringues filled with curd cheese,
fromage frais and a sharp lemon
curd surrounded by a light lemon
cream sauce

Trout poached in Dry Martini with a currant sauce, served with frisée

Don't forget the honey! It makes all
the difference. A good alternative is
to use the rind and juice of two
scrubbed oranges for a sauce which
I think works just as well, if not
better than with berries. If you use
oranges instead, remember to omit
the water and honey.

5 fl oz (150 ml) Dry Martini
2 bayleaves
1 onion, sliced
2 oz (50 g) redcurrants
Salt and pepper
1 tablespoon honey
2 whole trout
2 oz (50 g) blackcurrants
½ head frisée (curly endive)
1 tablespoon creamy fromage frais
Sherry vinegar, balsamic vinegar or
wine vinegar, to taste

Put the Dry Martini in a frying pan
with 5 fl oz (150 ml) water, the
bayleaves, sliced onion, redcurrants,
salt, pepper and honey and bring to
the boil. Remove the heads and tails
from the trout, and wash and pat dry.
Simmer the liquor and add the trout
to the pan. Cover and poach for about
7 minutes each side. Leave to cool a
little in the liquor. Then remove the
trout, skin and fillet them and place in
a shallow bowl. Meanwhile, add the
blackcurrants to the pan, reduce the
liquor and strain over the trout. Add
the bayleaves, then chill.

When ready to serve, arrange a bed
of frisée on each plate and place the
strips of trout on top. Whisk the
fromage frais into the liquor and taste
and adjust the seasoning. Sharpen, if
necessary, with a little vinegar. Then
strain and pour around the trout.

Fillet steak stuffed with mushrooms and seasonings with a wine sauce

Look for very good-quality fillet, making sure it's not too large, and pick the smallest button mushrooms that you can. Although it might seem unusual I always use a fruity white wine in this recipe rather than red because the flavour seems better and it prevents the sauce taking on that dark brown colour that you get with red wine.

5 oz (150 g) button mushrooms
1 oz (25 g) unsalted butter
1 clove garlic, crushed
1 tablespoon tomato purée
Salt and pepper
4 fillet steaks, about 1¼ in (3 cm) thick
4 fl oz (120 ml) white wine
10 fl oz (300 ml) chicken stock
2 teaspoons wholegrain mustard

Finely slice the mushrooms and sauté in half the butter, with the crushed garlic, until soft. Add the tomato purée and simmer until 'sticky'. Season with salt and pepper, and allow to cool. Then make a pocket in each steak and insert 1 large heaped teaspoon of the mushroom mixture. Refrigerate until ready to use.

Add the white wine and 5 fl oz (150 ml) chicken stock to the remaining mushroom mixture. Bring to a simmer and add more tomato purée if necessary, along with the wholegrain mustard. Taste and adjust the seasoning. If the sauce is too sticky, add more chicken stock.

When almost ready to serve, heat the remaining butter in a pan until very hot. Sear the steaks until cooked to your liking. Serve on hot plates with the Home-made parsleyed tagliatelle, cold Carrot salad and a little sauce on the side.

Home-made parsleyed tagliatelle

I picked up this idea of serving a piece of meat with pasta on an Austrian skiing trip and I think the combination is excellent.

7 oz (200 g) strong plain white flour
½ teaspoon salt
2 size 4 eggs
1 large knob unsalted butter
Freshly ground black pepper
2 tablespoons chopped fresh parsley

Place the flour, salt and eggs in a food processor with a metal blade and process until the mixture looks like granules. If it's a little dry, add some water and process again. Knead together, wrap in clingfilm and rest for about ½ hour. Cut the dough into 6 equal portions and put each piece through a pasta machine 2–3 times on the first setting to even out the pasta. Lay the dough on clean tea towels and repeat the process on the second setting. Keep rolling the dough in order on each setting down to the thinnest one on the pasta machine. If the pasta gets too unwieldy, cut it in half. Use a little flour, to dust, if the pan gets sticky.

When the dough is rolled to the thinnest setting, pass each piece through the tagliatelle cutter and hang up to dry on a clean broom handle or cane. Cut into manageable lengths and loosely roll up. Cover with a tea towel or clingfilm until ready to use so the pasta does not dry out too much or stick together. (At this point it can be frozen if you wish.)

When ready to cook, place the pasta in a pan of boiling salted water, bring back to the boil and cook for 2–3 minutes. Drain, but not too dry, add the butter, freshly ground black pepper and chopped parsley. Serve immediately. If cooking from frozen, do not put too much pasta in the pan as it will take too long to come back to the boil.

Carrot salad

This is an adaptation of a Madhur Jaffrey dish which I find a good salad to accompany cold meats at parties or barbecues. The black mustard seeds are a classic ingredient of Indian cuisine . . . try adding some sliced orange if you wish to vary the salad a bit.

1 lb (450 g) carrots
Salt and pepper
Juice of 1 lemon
1 tablespoon black mustard seeds

Scrape and wash the carrots and either shred them on a large shredder in a food processor or grate them by hand. Place in a bowl, season with salt and pepper and add the lemon juice. Heat a small heavy-based saucepan, add the mustard seeds and dry-roast them until they 'pop'. Add the roasted seeds to the carrot salad, mixing well. Refrigerate until ready to use.

Meringues filled with curd cheese, fromage frais and a sharp lemon curd surrounded by a light lemon cream sauce

This is my own recipe. One thing to note: if I'm going to keep the meringues for a few days I add a little cornflour to the last bit of sugar that I fold in to make them keep better.

2 size 4 eggs
3 oz (75 g) caster sugar, sifted together with 1 oz (25 g) icing sugar
2 lemons
1 teaspoon arrowroot
2 tablespoons caster sugar
4 oz (100 g) curd cheese
2–3 tablespoons creamy fromage frais
Sifted icing sugar, to decorate
10 fl oz (300 ml) half cream or 5 fl oz (150 ml) single cream and a little milk
A few sprigs of fresh lemon balm, to decorate

Separate the eggs and place the yolks in a heatproof glass bowl. Whip the whites with an electric beater until foamy, add half the mixed sugars and beat until very stiff. Gently fold in the remaining mixed sugars and place the mixture in an icing bag fitted with a plain ⅜ in (9.5 mm) nozzle. Line a baking tray with non-stick bakewell paper and pipe 8–10 × 3 in (7.5 cm) squares on to the paper. Dry the meringues in a very low oven.

Grate the rind from 1 lemon and add to the egg yolks. Remove the rind from the other lemon in long thin strips using a lemon zester, blanch in boiling water, refresh in cold water and set aside. Squeeze both lemons and add the juice to the yolks with a little arrowroot. Add 2 tablespoons caster sugar, mix well, place the bowl over a pan of hot water and stir until well thickened. Allow to cool and chill.

Now mix together the curd cheese and fromage frais and place in an icing bag fitted with a large six point nozzle. Pipe the mixture twice around the edges of 4 (or 5 if you have made 10) of the meringue squares. Fill with the cooled lemon curd and place the meringue lids on top. Dust generously with sifted icing sugar. Place a swirl of lemon rind at one corner of each meringue and put on a plate. Thin the remaining cooled lemon curd with enough cream to make a thin sauce. Pour some around each meringue and garnish with sprigs of lemon balm.

Round Three

JOAN BUNTING'S MENU

WINNER

•
STARTER
Salmon and asparagus mousse
•
MAIN COURSE
Rack of Northumbrian lamb
Potato puffs
Provençal green beans
•
DESSERT
Summer fruit tartlets

Salmon and asparagus mousse

The lemon sauce accompanying this mousse is a cheeky way of making hollandaise sauce and it's foolproof!

'A marriage made in heaven.'
PIERRE KOFFMANN

8 oz (225 g) fresh salmon fillets
2 eggs plus 2 egg yolks
5 fl oz (150 ml) double cream
Salt and pepper
1 bundle asparagus
4 oz (100 g) unsalted butter, melted and hot
Juice and finely grated rind of ½ lemon

Blend the salmon in a food processor until smooth. Add 1 egg and the cream, and season to taste with salt and pepper. Allow to cool, and chill. Meanwhile, cook the asparagus until tender. Reserve some of the tips as a garnish. Purée the remaining asparagus, add 1 egg and season with salt and pepper. Allow to cool, and chill.

Butter 4 moulds and divide half the salmon mixture between them. Each mould should be one-third filled. Add a layer of asparagus mousse and finish with salmon mousse. Cover with buttered greaseproof paper and cook in a shallow baking tray half-filled with water at gas mark 5, 375° F (190°C), for 25 minutes or until firm.

To make the sauce, melt the butter with the lemon rind, and season with salt and pepper. Blend the egg yolks and lemon juice in a blender, then add the hot butter in a steady stream until blended. Turn each mousse out and pour around some of the lemon sauce. Garnish with the asparagus tips.

Rack of Northumbrian lamb

Ideally, you should make deep cuts in the lamb, rub in the garlic, ginger and rum, and leave it overnight.

2 cloves garlic
1 oz (25 g) fresh ginger
3–4 tablespoons dark rum
1 rack of lamb, chined and scored
Salt and pepper
Juice of 1 orange

As far ahead as possible (the previous night if you can), purée the garlic and ginger in a blender and add the rum. Rub the mixture into the lamb, cover and refrigerate until ready to cook. Season the lamb with salt and pepper, cover the bone tips with foil to prevent browning and cook at gas mark 5, 375°F (190°C), for about 40 minutes, until just done. Allow the meat to rest for 5–10 minutes, then remove the foil. Blend the fresh orange juice with the pan juices, strain into a sauce boat and serve.

Potato puffs

1½ lb (750 g) potatoes
Salt and pepper
3 oz (75 g) butter
4 oz (100 g) plain white flour
3 eggs, beaten
Oil for deep frying.

Peel, boil and mash the potatoes, then season to taste with salt and pepper and allow to cool. To make the choux pastry, melt the butter in 4 fl oz (120 ml) water and bring to the boil. Add the flour and beat until smooth. Cool slightly, then add beaten egg until the dough is stiff and shiny. (You may not need to use all the eggs.) When both the mashed potato and the pastry are at room temperature, combine them in equal amounts (perhaps adding a little more potato). Heat the oil until it bubbles and drop in teaspoonfuls of the mixture. Fry until golden brown and puffed. Season lightly with salt and serve at once.

Provençal green beans

*8 oz (225 g) extra fine green beans,
topped and tailed
1 onion, chopped
1 clove garlic, chopped
1 tablespoon olive oil
2 large tomatoes, skinned and chopped
Salt and pepper
Chopped fresh parsley, to garnish*

Simmer the beans in salted water until just cooked. Drain and set aside. Soften the onion and garlic in the olive oil, add the tomatoes and cook gently until thickened. Add the drained beans, season with salt and pepper and stir until warmed through. Sprinkle with chopped parsley and serve.

Summer fruit tartlets

The wider the variety of fruit, the better – these tartlets look lovely on a summery table. Fill them as close to the time of serving as possible, otherwise they tend to go soggy.

*FOR THE PASTRY
8 oz (225 g) plain white flour
4 oz (100 g) butter, softened
4 oz (100 g) caster sugar
2 egg yolks
About 4 tablespoons milk, to mix*

*FOR THE FILLING
1 standard size carton fromage frais
Juice of 2–3 passion fruit, sieved
1–2 oz (25–50 g) caster sugar
About 1 lb (450 g) assorted fresh fruit
6–8 oz (175–225 g) apricot jam,
sieved and mixed with 2 tablespoons
water*

If you wish, the pastry can be prepared 24 hours in advance. Sift the flour into a mixing bowl and make a well in the centre. Place the butter, caster sugar, egg yolks and milk in the well and blend in gently, using your fingertips. Knead briefly and allow to rest in a cold place for at least 30 minutes. Line 4 × 4 inch (10 cm) tartlet tins with pastry and bake blind at gas mark 5, 375°F (190°C), for 15–20 minutes. Allow to cool.

For the filling, drain the fromage frais in a nylon sieve until thick. Blend in the passion fruit juice, and caster sugar to taste. Cover the base of the tartlet cases with this mixture and arrange a selection of fruit on top. Brush with the apricot glaze and serve.

CAROL ALEXANDER'S MENU

·
STARTER
Salad Alexandria
·
MAIN COURSE
Salmon and monkfish roast with orange and herb stuffing, served with ginger wine sauce
Saffron rice towers
Baked cherry tomatoes and courgette ribbons
·
DESSERT
Teacake and butter pudding with Cointreau cream

Salad Alexandria

2 × 1½ in (4 cm) thick slices white bread
2 oz (50 g) butter
1 clove garlic, crushed
Selected green leaves and herbs, for green salad
4 oz (100 g) oyster mushrooms
2 tablespoons olive oil
A pinch of salt
A pinch of dry mustard
1 teaspoon clear honey
Juice of ½ lime
4 thin slices Parma ham
4 quail's eggs
Lettuce, to garnish
4 tomato roses, to garnish

Trim the crusts off each slice of bread, then cut into 2 triangles. Melt the butter, add the crushed garlic and coat all sides of the triangles with the garlic butter mixture. Bake at gas mark 5, 375°F (190°C), for 15–20 minutes until golden on all sides. Carefully cut out the centre of each triangle and put the croûton 'baskets' back in the oven to dry out for a further 5 minutes. Leave to cool.

Make the salad from a selection of green leaves and herbs, then chop the oyster mushrooms. Make the dressing by putting the oil, salt, mustard, honey and lime juice in a screwtop jar with a tight-fitting lid. Shake well, then toss the salad, mushrooms and dressing together with your hands.

To assemble, fill each bread triangle with mixed salad. Cut julienne strips from the Parma ham and lay across the top of the salad in a lattice pattern. Poach the quail's eggs for 30 seconds and place on top of the ham. Garnish each plate with a lettuce leaf and a tomato rose.

Salmon and monkfish roast with orange and herb stuffing, served with ginger wine sauce

This is an easy way of cooking fish. It's what I call a 'meaty' fish dish because it has a fair bit of taste and texture to it. Get the fishmonger to remove the monkfish bones for you and keep them for the stock. The salmon and monkfish fillets must be approximately the same size.

About 1 lb (450 g) tail end of salmon, skinned and filleted
About 1 lb (450 g) top end of monkfish, skinned and filleted

FOR THE STUFFING
2 oz (50 g) butter
1 small onion, chopped
4 oz (100 g) breadcrumbs
3 tablespoons finely chopped fresh parsley
1 tablespoon finely chopped fresh lovage
Grated rind and juice of 1 small orange
A little crushed garlic
½ in (1 cm) piece of fresh ginger, chopped
Salt and pepper
2 medium free-range eggs (to give a better colour)
1 tablespoon olive oil

FOR THE SAUCE
¾ oz (20 g) butter
1 tablespoon plain white flour
5 fl oz (150 ml) fish stock
A little dry white wine
1–2 tablespoons green ginger wine
Salt and pepper

Cut the salmon and monkfish fillets in half horizontally, using a very sharp knife. Set aside.

To make the stuffing, melt the butter and fry the onion until soft. Remove from the heat and stir in the breadcrumbs. Add all the other stuffing ingredients except the orange juice, eggs and oil. Now beat the eggs and stir them in. Lay a salmon fillet down, spread some stuffing on top, place a monkfish fillet on top, then another layer of stuffing, then salmon, then stuffing, and a final layer of monkfish on top. Tie together at intervals with fine string. Wrap in foil. Squeeze the juice from the orange, add 1 tablespoon oil and pour over the fish. Bake at gas mark 4, 350°F (180°C), for 30–35 minutes. Cover and allow to stand for 10 minutes (this makes it easier to slice).

For the sauce, melt the butter in a pan, add the flour and cook together for 1 minute. Pour on the fish stock, white wine and green ginger wine to taste. Add the juices from the fish roast and season. Add a little more wine if the sauce is too thick.

Arrange the slices of fish on individual plates and serve the sauce separately.

Saffron rice towers

A few strands of saffron
6 oz (175 g) long-grain rice
Salt and pepper

Dissolve the saffron in a little boiling water. Wash the rice 4–5 times. Put it in a pan, add double the volume of water and the saffron. Bring to the boil, then simmer for 10 minutes. Check that the rice is tender. Drain and season with salt and pepper. Butter 4 moulds, pack the rice firmly into the moulds and place them in a roasting tin. Add hot water to the tin to a depth of ½ in (1 cm). Cover the moulds with greased foil and bake at gas mark 4, 350°F (180°C), for 25–30 minutes. When cooked, turn out on to individual plates and serve.

Baked cherry tomatoes and courgette ribbons

8 oz (225 g) cherry tomatoes
1 oz (25 g) butter
4 medium courgettes

Score round the centre of the cherry tomatoes. Brush with ½ oz (15 g) melted butter, place on a baking tray and bake at gas mark 5, 375°F (190°C), for 7–10 minutes depending on size. Cut the courgettes into long strips with a potato peeler. Place in a pan of boiling salted water, cook for 2 minutes and drain. Rinse with cold water. Then melt ½ oz (15 g) butter in a pan and add the courgette ribbons. Reheat for 1 minute only. Arrange decoratively to serve.

Teacake and butter pudding with Cointreau cream

I love bread and butter pudding, and this is my way of making it a little bit more special. The teacakes are light and soak up the liquid well. I use my own home-made jam but marmalade would also work well. In fact, you can put your own stamp on this dish by using your choice of jam.

'Excellent. Perfect.'
SIR TERENCE CONRAN

3 fl oz (85 ml) milk
4 fl oz (120 ml) double cream
A pinch of salt
1 large egg, beaten
2 oz (50 g) vanilla-flavoured sugar
2 large currant teacakes
1 oz (25 g) butter
Apricot and tangerine preserve or marmalade
A little sifted icing sugar, to dust

FOR THE CREAM
2 tablespoons apricot and tangerine preserve or marmalade
5 fl oz (150 ml) double or single cream
1 tablespoon Cointreau

Bring the milk, cream and salt to the boil, then allow to cool slightly. Mix the egg with the sugar, add the milk and cream mixture, then pour the custard mixture through a sieve. Cut the teacakes into thin slices and remove the crusts. Spread the slices with three-quarters of the butter and a little preserve or marmalade. Butter 4 ramekins and arrange slices of teacake in each one. Pour over the custard mixture and leave to soak for at least 20–30 minutes. Dot the remaining butter on top. Then place the ramekins in a baking tray containing enough water to come halfway up their sides. Cook at gas mark 3, 325°F (160°C), for 20–25 minutes. Allow to cool for 2–3 minutes, then turn out and dust the tops with sifted icing sugar.

To make the cream, heat the preserve or marmalade and push through a sieve. Allow to cool, then mix with the cream and Cointreau. If using single cream, flood each plate and serve the puddings on top. Double cream produces a thicker cream which could be served separately.

RICHARD SUTTON'S MENU

·

Scallop and king prawn 'sausage' with a lightly curried fish sauce

FOR THE SAUCE
1 shallot, chopped
A knob of butter
2 fl oz (50 ml) dry white wine
4 fl oz (120 ml) concentrated fish stock
2 tablespoons double cream
A pinch of curry powder

FOR THE 'SAUSAGE'
8 oz (225 g) firm white fish fillet (e.g. turbot, halibut or plaice)
1 egg white
2 tablespoons double cream
Salt and pepper
A pinch of cayenne pepper
4 oz (100 g) scallops
4 oz (100 g) shelled king prawns

First make the sauce. Sauté the shallot in the butter. Deglaze the pan with the white wine. Then add the fish stock and cook over a fairly high heat until reduced by half. Now add the cream and cook until thickened to a light coating consistency. Flavour with the curry powder and set aside.

To make the 'sausage', take a roasting bag and cut down the side and base to give a single plastic sheet. Lightly oil the sheet. Remove any remaining bones from the white fish and cut the fillet into chunks. Mince in a food processor for 30 seconds. Add the egg white and cream and process again until you have a firm mousse. Season to taste with salt, pepper and cayenne pepper.

Spread the mousse on the oiled plastic sheet, making a rectangular shape and leaving a gap of about 2 in (5 cm) around the edge. Place the scallops and prawns along the length of the rectangle of fish mousse. Now carefully roll the mousse up lengthways to enclose the scallops and prawns and form a fish 'sausage'. Seal the edges of the plastic sheet well and tie both ends firmly. Place inside another roasting bag and seal this well too. Steam or poach the 'sausage' in boiling water for no longer than 15 minutes. Feel to test for firmness.

When ready to serve, reheat the fish sauce. Carefully unwrap the 'sausage' and slice across to reveal the chunks of scallop and prawn. Arrange the slices on warmed plates and surround with some of the sauce.

Noisettes of lamb stuffed with field mushrooms and garlic

FOR THE LAMB
A knob of butter
3–4 large field mushrooms, coarsely chopped
2 cloves garlic, crushed
4 oz (100 g) fresh breadcrumbs
1 tablespoon double cream
Salt and pepper
1 rack of lamb, boned and trimmed
2–3 teaspoons fresh thyme leaves, and flowers if in season

FOR THE SAUCE
1 shallot, chopped
2 oz (50 g) butter
2 fl oz (50 ml) white wine vinegar
5 fl oz (150 ml) good chicken stock
Juices from the lamb, drained of fat

First make the stuffing. Heat the butter in a pan and sauté the mushrooms with 1 clove crushed garlic until dark and juicy. Add more butter if the mushrooms seem too dry. Now add 2 oz (50 g) breadcrumbs and mix well. Stir in the cream to bind the mixture, and season to taste with salt and pepper. Stuff the rack of lamb with the mushroom mixture, roll up and tie with string.

Mix the remaining 2 oz (50 g) breadcrumbs with 1 clove crushed garlic and the fresh thyme. Season with salt and pepper. Brush the rack of lamb with melted butter and roll it in the breadcrumb mixture. Place the lamb on a wire rack over a roasting tin and bake in a pre-heated oven at gas mark 8, 450°F (230°C), for 20–30 minutes, depending on the size of rack and your personal taste. Make sure the breadcrumb crust doesn't burn.

Meanwhile, make the sauce. Sweat the shallot in ½ oz (15 g) butter, then deglaze the pan with the vinegar. Reduce the liquid by half, add the chicken stock and lamb juices, and reduce a little more. Cut the remaining 1½ oz (40 g) butter into cubes and beat into the sauce off the heat.

When ready to serve, divide the rack into noisettes, arrange on individual plates and pour around some of the sauce. Accompany with a selection of lightly cooked vegetables.

Almond cream with caramel and apple sauce

*1 × 0.4 oz (11 g) sachet powdered
gelatine
3 egg yolks
5 oz (150 g) sugar
10 fl oz (300 ml) hot milk
4 oz (100 g) blanched whole almonds
2 fl oz (150 ml) apple juice
1 eating apple, peeled, cored and sliced
Clarified butter*

Put the gelatine in a bowl with 2 tablespoons hot water and leave to dissolve.

In a separate heatproof bowl, whisk the egg yolks and 3 oz (75 g) sugar until pale and thick. Gradually beat in the hot milk. Place the bowl over a pan of hot water and stir slowly over a moderate heat until thickened. (Don't allow to simmer as this will make the mixture curdle.) Whisk in the dissolved gelatine.

Place the almonds in a pre-heated oven at gas mark 8, 450°F (230°C), for 5–6 minutes. Grind them, fold into the cream mixture, strain, and spoon into small ramekins or moulds. Allow to cool, then refrigerate until set.

To make the sauce, put the remaining 2 oz (50 g) sugar in a pan with half the apple juice. Cook until coloured and caramelised. Remove from the heat, add the remaining apple juice to cool, and refrigerate until ready to serve.

Briefly sauté the slices of apple in clarified butter until coloured, then drain on kitchen paper. Turn each ramekin out on to an individual plate, surround with caramel sauce and decorate with apple slices.

THE REGIONAL HEATS

The South-West

BRIAN GLOVER'S MENU

WINNER

•
STARTER
Goat's cheese filos with salad and red pepper dressing
•
MAIN COURSE
John Dory with a saffron and orange sauce
Spinach with nutmeg
Carrots with coriander
•
DESSERT
Caramelised pears with ginger and lime syllabub and walnut and ginger biscuits

Goat's cheese filos with salad and red pepper dressing

Keep the filo pastry moist by covering it with a damp tea towel or a large polythene bag, and go easy on the dried tomatoes as they have quite a punchy flavour. Without the red pepper dressing these filos would make excellent canapés, although you should make them a bit smaller.

FOR THE PARCELS
6 oz (175 g) goat's cheese, de-rinded and cut into small dice
6 dried tomatoes in olive oil, chopped small
A few sprigs of fresh thyme, chopped
Black pepper
24 × 4 in (10 cm) squares filo pastry
3 oz (75 g) butter, melted
12 long chives

FOR THE SALAD AND DRESSING
1 clove garlic, lightly crushed
2 sprigs of fresh thyme, chopped
5 tablespoons extra virgin olive oil
1 tablespoon red wine vinegar
1 tablespoon chopped fresh basil
Salt, black pepper and sugar, to taste
1 red pepper
2 handfuls salad leaves (including
lettuce, rocket and watercress)

For the parcels, mix together the cheese, tomatoes and thyme, and season with pepper. Brush 12 filo squares with melted butter, lay the other 12 squares on top and brush those with butter too. Divide the cheese mixture between the 12 double squares and bring the pastry sheets up to form parcels, pinching to close. Tie each one with a chive, brush with melted butter and place on a greased baking tray. Bake at gas mark 5, 375°F (190°C), for 10–15 minutes.

To make the dressing, steep the garlic and thyme in the oil for at least 1 hour. Remove the garlic and make the dressing with the flavoured oil, vinegar, basil, salt, black pepper and sugar. Cut the red pepper in half, remove the seeds and place, skin side up, under a very hot grill until the skin has completely blackened. Remove the skin, cut the pepper into very fine dice and add to the dressing.

To serve, toss the leaves in the dressing and divide between 4 plates. Arrange 3 filo parcels on each plate next to the salad.

John Dory with a saffron and orange sauce

Fish is what I love to cook most. It demands to be cooked simply and you can do all your showing off around it. I cook this because John Dory is a good local fish and the accompanying sauce was inspired by the tastes of a fish stew I had while on holiday in Spain. Any flattish white fish would work well if John Dory was unavailable. Adapt it to whatever's best in the market. I would always serve this with good French bread for dipping in the sauce rather than potatoes or rice.

2 shallots, finely chopped
1 in (2.5 cm) piece fresh ginger, finely chopped
½ oz (15 g) butter
5 fl oz (150 ml) medium dry white wine
10 fl oz (300 ml) fish stock made from the bones of the fish
3 strips orange rind
A large pinch of saffron, soaked in 2 tablespoons hot fish stock
5–6 fl oz (150–175 ml) double cream
Salt and pepper
2 oz (50 g) unsalted butter, chilled
2 tablespoons finely chopped fresh coriander
2 medium-sized John Dory, filleted
A little melted butter
Orange segments, to garnish
A few fresh coriander leaves, to garnish

To make the sauce, fry the shallots and ginger for 5 minutes in ½ oz (15 g) butter in a small saucepan. Do not allow to brown. Add the wine, turn up the heat and reduce by half. Add the stock and reduce by about half again. Strain and return to the rinsed-out pan. Cut the orange rind into fine strands, blanch in boiling water for 5 minutes, then drain. Add the saffron and orange rind to the sauce and bring to the boil. Add the cream and boil until the sauce thickens a little. Taste and season with salt and pepper, then take the pan off the heat and whisk in the chilled butter, a little at a time, to thicken the sauce. Finally, add the chopped coriander.

Brush the fish with a little melted butter and season with salt and pepper. Grill for about 5 minutes. To serve, pour some sauce on 4 plates and place a fillet on each. Garnish with orange segments and coriander leaves. Serve with spinach and carrots.

Spinach with nutmeg

2 oz (50 g) butter
1½ lb (750 g) spinach, washed and picked over
Salt, pepper and ground nutmeg, to taste

Melt the butter in a large pan, add the spinach and cook, turning, over a medium heat until the leaves are tender and the liquid has been absorbed. Season to taste with salt, pepper and ground nutmeg.

Carrots with coriander

1 lb (450 g) carrots, cut into julienne strips
A knob of butter
A large pinch of brown sugar
1 teaspoon ground coriander
½ teaspoon finely grated orange rind
4 tablespoons orange juice
Salt

Blanch the carrots for 2 minutes in boiling water, then drain. Put them in a saucepan with the remaining ingredients and cook briskly until the carrots are tender and the liquid has been absorbed.

Caramelised pears with ginger and lime syllabub and walnut and ginger biscuits

It's worth making the biscuit dough well in advance. It will store in the fridge for about a week and in the freezer for up to a month. The good crunchy texture goes well with the pears, which should be served just warm, not chilled.

> *'The lime syllabub has lots of character. It's punchy.'*
> RICHARD SHEPHERD

FOR THE BISCUITS
4 oz (100 g) butter
4 oz (100 g) caster sugar
1 egg, beaten
6 oz (175 g) plain white flour
½ teaspoon ground ginger
A pinch of salt
3 oz (75 g) walnuts, chopped
2 pieces preserved ginger, chopped
A little milk (optional)

FOR THE SYLLABUB
Finely grated rind of 1 lime
Juice of ½ lime
A pinch of ground ginger
2 fl oz (50 ml) sherry
10 fl oz (300 ml) double cream
2 pieces preserved ginger, finely chopped
1–2 oz (25–50 g) caster sugar

FOR THE PEARS
2 oz (50 g) unsalted butter
4 large dessert pears, peeled, cored and sliced
2–3 tablespoons caster sugar
2 fl oz (50 ml) pear liqueur or brandy
A few strips of lime rind

To make the biscuits, cream the butter and sugar together until pale. Beat in the egg, then the flour sifted with the ground ginger and salt. Mix in the walnuts and preserved ginger. Bind to a stiff dough with a little milk if necessary. Form into a roll about 2 in (5 cm) in diameter and chill for several hours. Shave off thin biscuits from the roll and place on a greased baking tray. Bake at gas mark 5–6, 375–400°F (190–200°C) for about 10 minutes or until brown at the edges. Cool on a wire rack.

For the syllabub, put the lime rind, juice, ground ginger and sherry in a bowl. Leave to stand for at least 1 hour. Strain the mixture into a bowl, add the cream and whip until stiff. Fold in the chopped ginger, and sugar to taste. Chill until ready to serve.

To prepare the pears, melt the butter in a large frying pan. Add the pears and cook gently until tender. Raise the heat, add the caster sugar and cook until the pears caramelise. Add the liqueur or brandy and flambé.

To serve, arrange the pears on 4 plates. Put scoops of syllabub beside them, decorate with a few strips of lime rind and serve with the biscuits.

KATY MORSE'S MENU

.

Spinach and tomato roulade

FOR THE ROULADE
8 oz (225 g) cooked spinach
4 eggs, separated
2 oz (50 g) Gruyère cheese, grated
Salt and pepper

FOR THE SAUCE
¼ Spanish onion, finely chopped
2 tablespoons olive oil
1 clove garlic, unpeeled
1 lb (450 g) fresh ripe tomatoes,
skinned, de-seeded and finely chopped
2 tablespoons tomato purée
Salt and pepper
Lemon juice
½ oz (15 g) butter
2 tablespoons chopped fresh basil
Salad, to garnish

To make the roulade, purée the spinach, egg yolks and grated cheese in a blender. Season with salt and pepper. Then whisk the egg whites until stiff and fold into the spinach mixture. Put into a greased Swiss roll tin and bake at gas mark 5, 375°F (190°C), for 10–15 minutes until risen.

For the sauce, sauté the onion in the olive oil with the garlic clove until the onion is soft. Discard the garlic clove and add the tomatoes, tomato purée and 5 fl oz (150 ml) water. Simmer for 10 minutes and then blend until smooth. Season to taste with salt and pepper and lemon juice. Warm through, adding the butter and fresh basil.

To assemble, spread some of the sauce on the flat roulade and roll up into a long 'Swiss roll'. Cut into thick slices and serve on individual plates with more sauce and salad to garnish.

Roseland scallops

It's a good idea to cook an extra scallop to check whether or not they are done. I sometimes cook this as a starter rather than a main course, using three small scallops per person. The scallops should be as fresh as you can buy. A good test is that the flesh should move and spring back when you prod them.

FOR THE FLAKY PASTRY
9 oz (250 g) plain white flour
¼ oz (10 g) salt
11 oz (300 g) butter
5 fl oz (150 ml) ice-cold water

FOR THE FILLING
4 carrots
4 spring onions
1 in (2.5 cm) piece fresh ginger
1 oz (25 g) butter
24 scallops, cleaned
Salt and pepper
5 fl oz (150 ml) dry white wine
5 fl oz (150 ml) fish stock
5 fl oz (150 ml) double cream

To make the flaky pastry, sift the flour and salt into a large bowl. Rub in 2 oz (50 g) butter until the mixture resembles breadcrumbs. Then add just enough water to bind into a dough. Turn out on to a lightly floured board and knead until smooth. Roll out into a large rectangle, keeping the edges straight. Roll the remaining butter into a rectangle and place on the pastry. Fold into an envelope, turn 90° and then roll out carefully. Fold one third over another and repeat the process. Rest for 1 hour. Repeat the above process once more (so that the pastry has had 4 roll-outs each with 90° turns). The pastry is now ready to use.

Roll out the pastry and use a large scallop shell to press out 4 shell shapes. Mark with a knife to make them look like shells. Chill until required. Then bake blind at gas mark 7, 425°F (220°C), for 15 minutes.

Meanwhile, cut the carrots and spring onions into very fine julienne strips and grate the ginger. Sauté these ingredients in the butter in a large pan until they begin to soften. Add the scallops and season with salt and pepper. Once the scallops begin to change colour, add the white wine and stock and simmer for about 10 minutes until the scallops are just cooked. Remove the scallops and vegetables with a slotted spoon and keep warm. Turn the heat up high and reduce the liquid by half. Add the cream and simmer for 1 minute.

To assemble, place 1 scallop pastry shell on each plate and make a horizontal slit so that it opens like 2 hinged scallop shells. Arrange the scallops and vegetables inside and around each open shell. Pour the sauce around the plate but not on the pastry shell. Serve at once.

Almondine potatoes

Don't be tempted to add the chopped almonds to the mashed potato mixture as it makes the flavour too intense.

1 egg yolk
1 egg, beaten
Salt and pepper
1 lb (450 g) potatoes, boiled and mashed
Plain flour, to coat
3 oz (75 g) almonds, finely chopped

Add the egg yolk, half the beaten egg and the salt and pepper to the mashed potato. Shape the mixture into balls and chill until required. Coat the balls with flour, the remaining beaten egg and the chopped almonds. Chill for 30 minutes in the refrigerator. Then bake in a pre-heated oven at gas mark 5, 375°F (190°C), for 20 minutes.

Broccoli florets Parisienne

2 oz (50 g) butter
About 2 oz (50 g) breadcrumbs
2 tablespoons chopped fresh parsley
1 egg, hard-boiled and grated
Lemon juice
Salt and pepper
1 lb (450 g) broccoli, separated into
florets

Melt the butter and add all the remaining ingredients except the broccoli. Keep warm. Boil the broccoli until just cooked. Drain well and serve with the breadcrumb mixture sprinkled over the top.

Lime syllabub in brandysnap baskets

If you wanted you could use all wine instead of sherry in this dessert.

FOR THE BRANDYSNAP BASKETS
2 oz (50 g) caster sugar
2 oz (50 g) butter
2 oz (50 g) golden syrup
2 oz (50 g) plain flour
¼ teaspoon ground ginger
½ tablespoon brandy

FOR THE SYLLABUB
Juice and finely grated rind of 1 lime
2 fl oz (50 ml) sherry
1 fl oz (25 ml) brandy
2 oz (50 g) caster sugar
10 fl oz (300 ml) double cream,
lightly whipped
Fresh fruit (e.g. raspberries and kiwi
fruit), to garnish

To make the brandysnaps, gently melt the sugar, butter and syrup in a pan. Add the flour, ginger and brandy and stir well. Grease 2 baking sheets and put 2 large teaspoonfuls of the mixture, well spaced apart, on each baking sheet. Bake for about 5 minutes at gas mark 5, 375°F (190°C). The centre of each biscuit should be bubbling. Remove from the oven and allow to cool slightly. With a spatula, gently ease each biscuit off the tray and mould over a cup or orange to form a basket shape. Allow to cool.

To make the syllabub, put all the ingredients except the cream and fruit into a bowl. Stir until the sugar has melted. Then gradually beat in the cream until thick. Spoon the syllabub into the brandysnap baskets and garnish with fresh fruit such as raspberries and kiwi fruit.

ALAN SIM'S MENU

.

STARTER

A warm salad of scallops

.

MAIN COURSE

Roast best end of lamb with
olive-flavoured juices
Buttered spinach
Provençal vegetables

.

DESSERT

Crêpes with a passion fruit coulis

A warm salad of scallops

This is a salad to be eaten, not
looked at. A *salade tiède* should
always be warm, not hot, and it's
essential that the leaves are slightly
wilted. If you can, get the scallops
in their shells and alive, then they'll
survive in the fridge for at least 36
hours if you keep them in a plastic
bag.

12 large scallops
7 tablespoons extra virgin olive oil
Salt
Cayenne pepper
Lemon juice
1 tablespoon champagne vinegar or
good white wine vinegar
½ clove garlic
1 tablespoon finely chopped fresh herbs
(e.g. parsley and chives)
Freshly ground black pepper
4 handfuls prepared salad leaves
2 tablespoons roasted pine kernels

Clean the scallops, divide each white
noix into 2 rounds and shred the
corals. Heat 1 tablespoon olive oil in a
small pan until very hot. Toss the
shredded corals in the hot oil and
season with salt, cayenne pepper and
lemon juice. Reserve. Heat another
tablespoon olive oil in the pan until
smoking, add the white scallop
rounds, remove from the heat and
cover with foil. Warm the remaining 5
tablespoons olive oil, the vinegar, garlic and fresh herbs in the bottom of a
large saucepan. Season with salt and
freshly ground black pepper. Then
toss the salad leaves in the dressing
until they have lost their chill.

To serve, place the leaves in
warmed bowls. Top with the scallop
rounds and season with salt, lemon
juice and cayenne pepper. Garnish
with the pine kernels and fried
shredded corals.

Roast best end of lamb with olive-flavoured juices

This dish definitely needs the new season's lamb – the earlier in the year the better. Heavily trim the best end to get delicate little chops.
For me this dish bears out the Escoffier dictum, *'Faites simple'*. Everything should taste of what it is.

3½ fl oz (100 ml) vegetable oil
2 best ends of spring lamb, chined and 'frenched' (the bones chopped and reserved)
1 small onion, roughly chopped
1 small carrot, roughly chopped
8 fl oz (250 ml) veal stock
A sprig of fresh thyme
A piece of dried orange peel
½ teaspoon coarsely crushed black peppercorns
Salt and freshly ground black pepper
20 black Greek olives, blanched and stoned
A few drops of red wine vinegar

Heat half the vegetable oil in a roasting tin and toss the bones in the oil. When lightly coloured, add the onion and carrot. Transfer to a hot oven and bake at gas mark 7, 425°F (220°C), for 30 minutes or until the bones and vegetables are highly coloured. Pour off the oil and deglaze the pan with 8 fl oz (250 ml) water. Transfer the contents to a saucepan. Add the veal stock, thyme, orange peel and black peppercorns. Simmer for 20 minutes, skimming well, strain and reduce to about 7 fl oz (200 ml).

Heat the remaining vegetable oil in another roasting tin. Turn the best ends in the oil, searing all the surfaces. Season with salt and freshly ground black pepper, and roast at gas mark 7, 425°F (220°C), for about 15 minutes or until the internal temperature is 140°F (60°C). Leave the best ends to rest in a foil parcel for 15 minutes before serving.

Reheat the sauce, add the stoned olives and simmer gently to allow the flavour to infuse. Taste and correct the seasoning with salt, freshly ground black pepper and a few drops of red wine vinegar. To serve, carve the best ends into chops. Arrange on a bed of Buttered spinach with the sauce poured around, and accompany with Provençal vegetables.

Buttered spinach

Use best-quality unsalted butter such as Beurre de Charentes or Normandy butter.

1 lb (450 g) dark-leaved young spinach
2 oz (50 g) sweet unsalted butter
Salt and freshly ground black pepper

Blanch the spinach in boiling salted water, then refresh in cold water. Drain well and place in a pan with the other ingredients. Heat for 1 minute, then serve.

Provençal vegetables

I first made this last year for a barbecue and it's literally a disassembled ratatouille. I serve it in a copper gratin dish because it seems to improve the appearance of the vegetables and give them a rustic look. If you use dried rather than fresh thyme, use considerably less, otherwise the dish will be too herby.

'This is very butch food.'
MICHAEL CAINE
'Sort of Rambo goes to Provence.'
LOYD GROSSMAN

2 small courgettes, sliced and blanched
2 peppers, roasted, peeled, quartered and de-seeded
1 small aubergine, sliced and fried in extra virgin olive oil
A bunch of fresh thyme
1 bulb garlic, peeled and cloves blanched for 20 minutes
Salt and freshly ground black pepper

Place the vegetables in an ovenproof dish. Scatter over the thyme and garlic cloves and season with salt and freshly ground black pepper. Dribble over the oil previously used to cook the aubergines. Then bake at gas mark 7, 425°F (220°C), for 15 minutes before serving.

Crêpes with a passion fruit coulis

This is a very simple recipe based on a crêpe suzette but served with an interesting passion fruit coulis rather than being laden with alcohol. For a good strong passion fruit flavour you could use 12–15 passion fruit and reduce the orange juice accordingly.

FOR THE CRÊPES
4 oz (100 g) plain flour
A pinch of salt
1 egg plus 1 egg yolk
1 teaspoon sugar
1 teaspoon melted butter
10 fl oz (300 ml) milk
Butter, for frying

FOR THE COULIS AND GARNISH
8 passion fruit
Juice and rind of 1½ oranges
2 oz (50 g) sugar
2 fl oz (50 ml) Maraschino
2 fl oz (50 ml) Cointreau

Make a batter in the usual manner. Melt a little butter in a small frying pan, pour in a small amount of the batter and swirl round to cover the bottom of the pan. When cooked on one side, slide a spatula underneath, flip over and cook on the other side. Repeat with the rest of the batter. This recipe should make about 8–10 crêpes.

For the coulis, cut the passion fruit in half. Scoop out the pulp and place in a food processor with the orange juice. Whiz for 1 minute to free the passion fruit pulp from the seeds. Strain through a fine sieve into a saucepan, bring to the boil, skimming well, and reserve.

For the garnish, cut the orange rind into fine julienne strips and blanch in boiling water for 8 minutes. Put the sugar in a pan with 2 fl oz (50 ml) water. Heat until it forms a sugar syrup, then add the orange rind and cook until it caramelises. Reserve.

To serve, place half the coulis in a large pan and warm 1 of the crêpes in the sauce. Fold into 4. Repeat until you have warmed 4 crêpes in the sauce. Pour over half the Maraschino and Cointreau. Repeat the operation with the other 2 servings. Serve each person with 2 crêpes scattered with strips of caramelised orange rind.

Wales

·
STARTER
White Cheshire salad with
coriander

·
MAIN COURSE
Tikka-style turkey with
basmati rice
Camembert-baked peppers with
green chillies and soured cream
Spicy red beans with cumin seeds

·
DESSERT
Sharp orange fool with kumquats,
fresh ginger and Cointreau

White Cheshire salad with coriander

2 slices white bread
1 clove garlic, crushed
5–6 tablespoons olive oil
1 tablespoon white wine vinegar
A dash of mustard oil (optional)
Salt
A pinch of cayenne pepper
1 head Lollo Rosso lettuce, separated
into leaves
1 bunch frisée (curly endive)
6 oz (175 g) White Cheshire cheese
Coriander leaves, to garnish

First make the garlic croûtons. Trim the crusts off the bread and cut into ½ in (1 cm) squares. Put the garlic in a frying pan with 2–3 tablespoons olive oil. When the oil begins to bubble, throw in the bread. Fry quickly, stirring, for a few minutes until golden. Drain on kitchen paper and set aside.

To make the dressing, put the remaining 3 tablespoons olive oil, vinegar, mustard oil if using, salt and cayenne pepper in a glass screwtop jar with a tight-fitting lid. Shake well before use.

Put the Lollo Rosso in a bowl, toss with 2 tablespoons dressing and place in a large dish. Slice the frisée into shorter lengths and arrange in the centre. Sprinkle on the croûtons and crumble over the cheese. Warm the remaining dressing in a pan, then pour over the salad. Garnish with a few coriander leaves.

Tikka-style turkey

I usually buy an 8 lb (3.5 kg) turkey, remove the breast, cut it into cubes and use the rest of the turkey to make curries.

FOR THE MARINADE
About 15 fl oz (450 ml) natural yoghurt
3 tablespoons sunflower oil
1 rounded teaspoon salt
2 tablespoons finely chopped fresh ginger
6 cloves garlic, crushed
1–2 teaspoons cayenne pepper
Juice of 1 lemon

About 2 lb (1 kg) turkey breast, cut into 1 in (2.5 cm) cubes
1 large red pepper and 1 large green pepper, de-seeded and cut into 1 in (2.5 cm) squares
8 oz (225 g) baby onions, cut into quarters

Mix all the marinade ingredients together in a large bowl. Add the turkey breast cubes to the marinade, stirring well. Cover and refrigerate for an absolute minimum of 8 hours. Thread on to skewers with squares of red and green pepper and onion quarters. Grill, turning when golden, for 15–20 minutes. Keep checking to make sure they don't get overcooked. Serve with basmati rice.

Camembert-baked peppers with green chillies and soured cream

2 onions, sliced into thin rings
1 tablespoon sunflower oil
6 firm red, green and yellow peppers, de-seeded and thinly sliced lengthways
½–1 green chilli, finely chopped
1 tablespoon tomato purée
Salt and pepper
1 × 5 fl oz (150 ml) carton soured cream
½ Camembert, de-rinded and roughly chopped

Gently fry the onion in the sunflower oil. Do not allow to brown. When the onion is soft, remove it from the pan with a slotted spoon and reserve. Turn the heat up and stir-fry the peppers for several minutes until they begin to soften. Reduce the heat and add the chilli. Continue to stir-fry for 2 minutes. Return the onion to the pan with 2 fl oz (50 ml) water and the tomato purée. Simmer for about 5 minutes, until the liquid has reduced a little. Season with salt and pepper, then stir in the soured cream and chopped Camembert. Transfer to a pre-heated ovenproof dish and bake for 20 minutes at gas mark 5, 375°F (190°C), until it begins to bubble.

Spicy red beans with cumin seeds

This is my own invention but it still turns out different every time. Roasting the spices really does improve the flavour. Try to add the yoghurt very slowly, otherwise it will go grainy.

1 bayleaf
1 teaspoon coriander seeds
1 teaspoon cumin seeds
Seeds from 2 cardamom pods
3 cloves
1 in (2.5 cm) cinnamon stick
1 tablespoon ground coriander
2 tablespoons ground cumin
1 heaped teaspoon paprika (optional)
1 large onion, thinly sliced
3 × 15 oz (425 g) tins red kidney beans, rinsed
3 cloves garlic, crushed
½–1 green chilli, finely chopped
2 tablespoons sunflower oil
1 × 15 oz (425 g) tin chopped plum tomatoes
5 fl oz (150 ml) natural yoghurt
Salt and black pepper
1 teaspoon sugar

Roast the bayleaf, coriander seeds, cumin seeds, cardamom seeds, cloves and cinnamon in a frying pan without oil. Heat over a medium flame until they begin to smell beautiful. Allow the spices to cool, then place in a blender or coffee mill with the ground coriander and cumin, and the paprika if using. Add half the onion and about two-thirds of the kidney beans and blend or process to a paste. Gently fry the remaining onion, garlic and green chilli in the oil until softened but not browned. Add the blended ingredients and fry quite vigorously for 2–3 minutes. (Add more oil if the mixture is too dry.) Add the remaining beans, stir in the tomatoes and simmer. Gradually add the yoghurt and continue to simmer until the sauce thickens considerably. Add salt, black pepper and a good teaspoon of sugar, or to taste.

Sharp orange fool with kumquats, fresh ginger and Cointreau

I made this up on my application form for the *MasterChef* competition – I'd never tried it out before but luckily it worked. Be very careful not to overwhip the cream before you blend in the rest of the mixture.

'I could eat the whole of that – I'd like the recipe, please.'
EDWINA CURRIE

1 pint (600 ml) double cream
4 oranges, rind, pith and pips removed, and cut into thick slices
10 kumquats, pips removed, or an extra orange
2½ tablespoons caster sugar
3 tablespoons Cointreau
Rind and juice of 1 large unwaxed lemon
1 teaspoon very finely chopped fresh ginger

Whip the cream until it begins to thicken and will form soft peaks. Put the oranges in a blender or food processor with 9 of the kumquats, 1½ tablespoons caster sugar and the Cointreau. Blend or process until a thick purée is formed.

Shred about 2 teaspoons lemon rind. Place in a bowl with the chopped ginger, 1 level tablespoon caster sugar and the lemon juice. Mix well.

Now divide the whipped cream between the lemon bowl and another bowl, putting slightly less in the lemon bowl. Fold the lemon mixture into the cream. Reserve 2 tablespoons orange purée and fold the rest into the remaining cream.

To serve, layer the 2 creams into dishes or large wine glasses, beginning with the lemon. Top with the remaining orange purée and decorate with a twisted slice of kumquat or orange.

MARTIN BENTON'S MENU

•
STARTER
Baked salmon with cucumber and a lemon cream sauce
•
MAIN COURSE
New Welsh broth
•
DESSERT
Cinnamon puddings with cider sauce and apples

Baked salmon with cucumber and a lemon cream sauce

It's definitely worth getting hold of white port for this dish, as it has so much more body than white wine. You don't need to oil the gratin dishes because there is plenty of moisture in the salmon and cucumber to prevent them from sticking.

1 cucumber
Salt
2 oz (50 g) unsalted butter, diced
4 × 4½ oz (120 g) salmon fillets
White pepper
Finely grated rind and juice of 1 lemon
1 in (2.5 cm) piece fresh ginger, peeled and finely grated
2 shallots, finely chopped
3 fl oz (85 ml) white port
3 fl oz (85 ml) double cream
Cayenne pepper
Chopped fresh parsley, to garnish

Top, tail, peel and halve the cucumber lengthways. Scrape out the central core of 'pips'. Slice into semicircles, put in a colander, sprinkle with salt and leave for about 30 minutes. Chill 1 oz (25 g) butter. Season the 4 pieces of salmon with salt, white pepper, a little finely grated lemon rind and a little grated ginger. Place each piece in the centre of a gratin dish. Wash and dry the cucumber halves and arrange around the salmon. Sprinkle the salmon with a little lemon juice. Then wrap each gratin dish in baking foil, ensuring that there is a pocket of air above the salmon and that the foil is well sealed.

Soften the shallots in the remaining 1 oz (25 g) butter. Add 3 fl oz (85 ml) lemon juice and the port, reduce by half and set aside. Heat the oven to gas mark 9, 475°F (240°C), or hotter if possible. Bake the salmon for 10 minutes. Now reheat the lemon and port reduction, add the cream and let it reduce slightly.

Whisk in the chilled diced butter. Season with salt, white pepper, cayenne pepper and some ginger.

To serve, remove the foil from the salmon dishes and use kitchen paper to wipe away any juices which may have been released. Pour some sauce on either side of the salmon and cucumber arrangement and garnish with a little parsley down the length of the salmon pieces.

New Welsh broth

I'm a great lamb fan, and I'm extremely happy to be within reach of the best lamb in the world! This is an adaptation of cawl, a traditional Welsh dish, although both Paul Bocuse and Anton Mosimann do similar versions. Do take your confidence in both hands and only poach the lamb for 5 minutes. Don't give it any longer, but it must stand for at least 10 minutes afterwards. Stand it on a small plate, placed upside down on a larger one. This allows the juices to run down for you to collect, and stops the meat standing in its own juices.

2 loins or best ends neck of lamb (10-12 chops in all)

FOR THE STOCK
½ onion, chopped
½ leek, chopped
1 stick celery, chopped
1 oz (25 g) unsalted butter
Salt
10 black peppercorns

FOR THE VEGETABLES
3 oz (75 g) leeks
3 oz (75 g) red onions
3 oz (75 g) Spanish onions
4 red cabbage leaves
8 Savoy cabbage leaves
2 oz (50 g) unsalted butter
Salt and pepper
2 cloves garlic
1 tablespoon snipped fresh chives
1 teaspoon snipped fresh basil
20 medium new potatoes

Ask your butcher to remove the fat and take the meaty 'eyes' out of the lamb joints, or do it yourself. Keep the remaining bones and meat trimmings.

To make the stock, sweat the chopped vegetables in the butter. Add the lamb bones and trimmings and brown lightly. Add salt to taste, and the peppercorns. Cover with 1¾ pints (1 litre) water and simmer, uncovered, for 45 minutes. Strain and reduce to about 10 fl oz (300 ml).

Now slice the leeks down their length and cut into 1–2 in (2.5–5 cm) pieces. Quarter the onions. Then separate the leeks and onions into their natural layers, and cut the cabbage leaves into 2–3 in (5–7.5 cm) pieces. Soften the leeks and onions in 1 oz (25 g) butter. Add the cabbage leaves and season with salt and pepper. Put the lamb on top of the vegetables, pour over the stock and bring to the boil. Cover the pan and simmer for 5 minutes only.

Transfer the meat to a warm dish, cover with foil and leave to rest in a cool oven at gas mark ¼, 225°F (110°C). Peel the garlic cloves and halve them lengthways. Add the garlic, 1 teaspoon chives and the basil to the vegetables. Cover and keep warm. Slice the lamb, adding any juices to the broth. Remove the garlic and stir in 1 oz (25 g) butter.

To serve, divide the vegetables and broth between 4 plates, arrange the meat slices on top and sprinkle over 1 teaspoon chives. Boil the potatoes in their skins and toss in butter. Serve in separate dishes, garnished with the remaining chives.

Cinnamon puddings with cider sauce and apples

This recipe is virtually foolproof. Don't blanch the orange rind as it adds to the flavour, and try to get the best-quality cider you can lay your hands on for the sauce. The puddings will sit for a short while, but the sooner they get on to the table, the lighter and fluffier they will be.

'If Kim Basinger were a pudding . . .'
LOYD GROSSMAN
'. . . but it wouldn't last nine and a half weeks . . .'
EDWINA CURRIE

FOR THE SAUCE AND APPLES
1 large orange
1 lemon
2 large Cox's apples
4 in (10 cm) cinnamon stick
2 cloves
15 fl oz (450 ml) strong dry cider
3 oz (75 g) caster sugar

FOR THE PUDDINGS
5 oz (150 g) unsalted butter
3 oz (75 g) caster sugar
3 eggs
2½ oz (65 g) ground almonds
1 teaspoon ground cinnamon
3 oz (75 g) self-raising flour
2 tablespoons Calvados
Dried white breadcrumbs, to coat moulds

Thinly peel the rind from the orange and cut into fine strips. Squeeze half the orange and half the lemon. Peel the apples, halve, core, and cut each half into 8 segments. Keep the apple segments covered in lemon juice to avoid discoloration.

Put the orange and lemon juice, cinnamon stick, cloves, cider and caster sugar into a large saucepan. Bring to a simmer and add the apple segments. Poach the apple pieces for about 5 minutes, until just tender. Remove the apple segments with a slotted spoon and reserve. Add the orange rind strips to the remaining liquid and reduce to a light syrup. Remove the cinnamon and cloves and leave to cool.

To make the puddings, cream the butter and half the sugar. Separate the eggs. Beat the yolks into the butter and sugar. Mix in the almonds, ground cinnamon, flour and Calvados. Beat the egg whites with the remaining sugar. Fold into the pudding mixture. Butter 4 individual ramekins or moulds and coat with the breadcrumbs. Spoon the mixture into the moulds, stand them in a roasting tray filled with water to a depth of ¾–1¼ in (2–3 cm) and bake at gas mark 4, 350°F (180°C), for 25–30 minutes.

To serve, unmould the puddings on to separate plates. Surround each with 8 apple segments. Pour a little of the cider syrup around, spreading the strips of rind around each plate.

MARY FERRIS'S MENU

·
STARTER
Surprise salmon mousse
·
MAIN COURSE
Medallions of Welsh lamb with a redcurrant, green peppercorn and honey glaze
Laverbread tarts
Fresh vegetables
·
DESSERT
Chocolate glory

Surprise salmon mousse

You have to take your time over this recipe. In particular, if you add the cream too fast the mixture can curdle. When cooking the mousse don't be afraid to prod it with your fingers to test it, because it's horrible if overcooked.

FOR THE MOUSSE
8 oz (225 g) salmon fillets, skinned
3 eggs
15 fl oz (450 ml) double cream
2 oz (50 g) smoked salmon pieces, chopped
Salt and pepper

FOR THE SAUCE
2 leeks, finely chopped
A knob of butter
5 fl oz (150 ml) double cream
A pinch of nutmeg
Salt and pepper
½ oz (15 g) sunflower seeds

Cut the salmon fillets into cubes and whiz in a food processor using the metal blade. Add the eggs, 1 at a time, processing for about 1 minute each time. Chill the mixture. Return the bowl to the processor and trickle in the cream, using the pulse control to stop it curdling. Fold in the chopped smoked salmon and season with salt and pepper. Spoon the mixture into 4 buttered ramekins, cover with clingfilm and refrigerate. When ready to cook, place in a roasting tin containing enough boiling water to come three-quarters of the way up the sides of the ramekins. Bake in a pre-heated oven at gas mark 5, 375°F (190°C), for 30 minutes.

For the sauce, steam the chopped leeks until tender. Blend in a food processor or blender with the butter, cream, nutmeg, salt and pepper. Keep warm.

Pour some sauce on to each plate, turn out a hot mousse in the centre, sprinkle with sunflower seeds and serve immediately.

Medallions of Welsh lamb with a redcurrant, green peppercorn and honey glaze

You should be able to find raspberry vinegar in your local supermarket (don't use malt or cider vinegars as they are much too harsh). Fresh laverbread is widely available in Wales, and tins of it are sold in many good delis throughout Britain.

'Dream farmhouse food . . . I imagine the Archers sitting down to this . . .'
LOYD GROSSMAN

FOR THE SAUCE
1 large onion, finely chopped
1 teaspoon green peppercorns, crushed
A little sunflower oil
4 oz (100 g) fresh or frozen redcurrants, thawed if frozen
½ pint (300 ml) lamb stock
1 tablespoon raspberry vinegar
Salt and freshly ground black pepper

FOR THE MEDALLIONS
2 small best ends neck of lamb, filleted
Salt and pepper
Butter and sunflower oil, to pan-fry
½ teaspoon honey

To make the sauce, sweat the onion with the crushed green peppercorns in a little sunflower oil. Add the redcurrants, the stock and vinegar, and simmer for at least 20 minutes until the sauce has thickened. Blend or process and pass through a sieve. Season with salt and freshly ground black pepper, thicken if necessary and keep warm.

Now cut the fillet into medallions about ¾ in (2 cm) thick and season with salt and pepper. Pan-fry in a little butter and sunflower oil, allowing 3–4 medallions per person. When cooked, brush a little honey on each and glaze under a hot grill.

To serve, pour the sauce on to one half of the plate, arrange the medallions on top and place the laverbread tart and vegetables to one side.

Laverbread tarts

Laverbread is a seaweed that comes from the rocks on the West Wales coast. Traditionally, it's mixed with oatmeal, made into little cakes, fried, and eaten for breakfast with cockles and bacon.

2½ oz (65 g) butter
4 oz (100 g) plain white flour
Salt and pepper
5 oz (150 g) laverbread
Grated rind and juice of 1 orange
2 cloves garlic, crushed

Rub 2 oz (50 g) butter into the flour with a pinch of salt until the texture resembles fine breadcrumbs. Add 1½ tablespoons ice-cold water and gently mix together to form a dough. Line 4 deep tart cases with the pastry, cover the base of each with baking beans and bake blind in a pre-heated oven at gas mark 6, 400°F (200°C), for 8–10 minutes. Remove the baking beans and cook for a further 3 minutes.

Heat the laverbread, orange rind and juice, garlic, ½ oz (15 g) butter, and salt and pepper in a pan. When the pastry cases are cooked, fill them with the laverbread mixture and keep warm.

Fresh vegetables

16 new potatoes
Chopped fresh parsley
8 oz (225 g) baby carrots
½ oz (15 g) butter
1 tablespoon sugar
8 oz (225 g) tiny courgettes, sliced
Sunflower oil, to stir-fry
Salt and pepper

Steam the new potatoes until tender, then roll in finely chopped parsley. Cook the baby carrots in boiling salted water for 5 minutes. Melt the butter and sugar together in a pan, then add the carrots and cook, stirring, for a further 5 minutes. Stir-fry the sliced courgettes in very hot oil for 2–3 minutes. Season all the vegetables with salt and pepper and serve.

Chocolate glory

'This ought to be licensed!'
EDWINA CURRIE

4 oz (100 g) dried apricots, chopped
Grated rind and juice of 1 orange
4 oz (100 g) caster sugar
8 oz (225 g) ricotta cheese
4 oz (100 g) good-quality plain
chocolate, broken into squares
Cointreau, to taste
A few crushed macaroon biscuits, to
decorate

Put the chopped apricots and grated orange rind in a pan with enough water to cover. Simmer until tender. Blend or process the caster sugar and ricotta cheese together until light and creamy. Put the orange juice in a small pan, add the chocolate and heat gently until the chocolate melts. Blend or process the apricot mixture. When cool, add to the sweetened ricotta, with Cointreau to taste. Then fold in the melted chocolate. Dish up into tall glasses and decorate with crushed macaroons.

The Midlands

SUSAN COWLEY'S MENU

.
STARTER
Cream of celery soup
.
MAIN COURSE
West Country beef rolls
.
DESSERT
Tarte Louise

Cream of celery soup

This recipe in some ways is wrongly named. Celery is just one of many flavours that go into it. It's quite old-fashioned in the sense that it relies heavily on its stock. Really take time over the stock – I'm afraid there are no short cuts on this one. When the stock is cold it must be so concentrated that it becomes like jelly. Brandy sharpens up the taste which can be quite bland if you're not careful.

FOR THE STOCK
2 chicken carcasses
2 leeks
2 onions
2 carrots
3 bayleaves
1 bunch of fresh thyme
3 stalks of fresh parsley (with their leaves)

FOR THE SOUP
½ oz (15 g) butter
2 cloves garlic, sliced
4 sticks celery, chopped
2 pints (1.2 litres) chicken stock
2 potatoes, boiled and sieved
Salt and pepper
2 tablespoons brandy
2 tablespoons single cream

To make the stock, place the chicken carcasses, vegetables and herbs in a large pan. Add water to cover, bring to the boil and simmer for 3–4 hours, adding more water if necessary to maintain the liquid level. Strain to remove the solids and reserve.

For the soup, melt the butter in a pan and fry the garlic on a very low heat for approximately 5 minutes. Remove the garlic, add the celery and fry gently until soft on the outside. Add the stock and sieved potato, and season with salt and pepper. Bring to the boil and simmer for about 15 minutes. Add the brandy and cream, adjust the seasoning and serve.

West Country beef rolls

This is an adaptation of a dish made by a friend's Cornish auntie. It makes a good heartening winter meal. It's really a sort of beef olives *en daube*. Make sure that when you beat the steak you beat the edges well. If you leave thick edges you'll have difficulty rolling it up. It's also best to cook it in a tall pot with several layers of vegetables, wine and beef rolls. If you have to use a shallow dish, cover it with greaseproof paper, otherwise the meat will dry out. Serve it with new potatoes and broccoli to add a bit of colour.

6 oz (175 g) sausage meat
1 tablespoon chopped fresh parsley
1 teaspoon chopped fresh thyme
3 onions, 1 chopped and 2 sliced
2 cloves garlic, chopped
Salt and pepper
4 large slices beef topside
Beef dripping
4 carrots, sliced
2 sticks celery, sliced
1 tablespoon flour
10 fl oz (300 ml) red wine
10 fl oz (300 ml) beef stock
1 teaspoon tomato purée

Put the sausage meat in a bowl, add the chopped herbs, 1 chopped onion, 1 clove garlic and salt and pepper. Mix well and reserve. Beat out the pieces of beef and cut into 8–10 × 4 in (10 cm) squares. Put a spoonful of sausage meat mixture on to each beef square, fold the sides over and roll up. Secure each beef roll with string.

Heat the beef dripping in a frying pan. Fry the rolls until sealed, then transfer to a casserole dish. Add 2 sliced onions, 1 clove garlic, the carrots and celery to the dripping. Fry until soft on the outside. Add the flour and stir for 1 minute. Add the wine, stock and tomato purée. Season with salt and pepper, and stir constantly until boiling. Add the sauce to the casserole, cover and bake at gas mark 4, 350° (180°), for 1½ hours.

To serve, remove the string from the beef rolls and arrange them on a serving dish with the vegetables. Reduce the sauce until thick and pour over the beef and vegetables.

Tarte Louise

This is named after my daughter. It was invented when I was going to do Normandy tart and, having made the filling, I realised that I didn't have any eating apples for the top. This dish really is very easy. When you make the trellis pattern on the top, place each piece of pastry at right angles to the next one. If you try and weave it you'll get pastry everywhere! When you sprinkle the cinnamon and sugar it's easy to get it thicker in some places than others, in which case it won't melt and go brown because the apple juice doesn't get soaked up. If this happens, melt some butter, drip it over the dry patches with a pastry brush and return it to the oven for a couple of minutes. Try to use Bramley cookers, as they disintegrate well and purée better than other apples.

FOR THE PASTRY
6 oz (175 g) plain white flour
3 oz (75 g) butter, softened
3 teaspoons caster sugar
1 egg yolk
2 tablespoons cold water

FOR THE FILLING
1 lb (450 g) cooking apples
4 oz (100 g) caster sugar
½ oz (15 g) butter
A little lemon juice
4 tablespoons soft brown sugar
1 tablespoon cinnamon

To make the pastry, sift the flour on to a clean work surface. Rub in the butter, then make a well in the centre and add the sugar, egg yolk and water. Knead together to form a dough and roll out. Line a flan dish with the pastry and prick the base lightly with a fork. Reserve the pastry trimmings.

For the filling, peel, core and roughly chop the apples. Put them in a pan with 1 tablespoon water, the caster sugar, butter and lemon juice, and cook until tender. Whisk to purée. Allow to cool, then pour into the flan case. Mix the soft brown sugar with the cinnamon and sprinkle on top of the apple. Roll the remaining pastry into long pieces and arrange in a lattice pattern on top of the tart. Bake at gas mark 6, 400°F (200°C), for 30 minutes.

ANTHONY HAROLD'S MENU

·
STARTER
Mediterranean prawns with garlic butteu
·
MAIN COURSE
Filet de boeuf en croûte
Gratin dauphinois
Sauce hollandaise
·
DESSERT
Crêpe soufflé on raspberry coulis

Mediterranean prawns with garlic butter

This is my all-time favourite starter. Try to get fresh rather than frozen prawns, although a word of warning: they're extremely hard to find and when you do find them they're wickedly expensive.

4–6 oz (100-175 g) butter
2–3 cloves garlic, crushed
20–25 Mediterranean prawns
Chopped fresh parsley, to garnish
Lemon juice

Melt the butter and garlic together in a pan. Put the prawns in a steamer and heat over boiling water for 5–6 minutes.

To serve, divide the garlic butter between 4 ramekin dishes and set these on plates. Surround each ramekin with prawns. Garnish with chopped parsley, and finish with a squeeze of lemon juice.

Filet de boeuf en croûte

If you're buying rather than making puff pastry, look for the fresh chilled rather than frozen stuff. It's better than the frozen pastry and comes in larger quantities. The stuffing must be kept on the heat until the juice has completely evaporated.

1–1½ lb (450-750 g) piece fillet steak
A little brandy
3 oz (75 g) butter
8 oz (225 g) open flat mushrooms
4 oz (100 g) shiitake mushrooms
1 large onion, finely chopped
Salt and pepper
1 lb (450 g) ready-made puff pastry
1 egg, beaten (optional)

Trim any fat off the beef. Brush with brandy, dot with 1 oz (25 g) butter and bake at gas mark 7, 425°F (220°C), for about 15 minutes. Remove and leave to cool. (This initial cooking time really depends on how well you like your steak cooked. It needs to be almost cooked, as it is going to be finished off in the pastry case.)

Meanwhile, wipe the mushrooms with kitchen paper and chop finely. Sauté the chopped onion in the remaining 2 oz (50 g) butter for 5 minutes over a low heat. Add the chopped mushrooms and stir well. Now cook, uncovered, over a low heat for about 10 minutes. Stir occasionally to let all the juices evaporate, until you have a concentrated mixture. Season with salt and pepper.

Roll the pastry into a rectangle. Spread with half the mushroom mixture in an even layer, leaving a gap of about 2 in (5 cm) around the edges. Place the cooled steak on top of the mushrooms but do not press down. Spread the rest of the mushroom mixture over the steak and carefully wrap the pastry around the meat, very loosely. (If the pastry is too tightly wrapped, the air cannot circulate and the mushroom mixture oozes out.) Place the pastry 'parcel' on a greased baking tray, join side down, and decorate with pastry trimmings cut into leaf shapes. Brush with beaten egg or salt water. Bake at gas mark 6, 400°F (200°C), for 30 minutes, reducing the temperature to gas mark 5, 375°F (190°C), if the pastry starts to brown too quickly.

To serve, a hollandaise sauce complements the beef beautifully. Gratin dauphinois and mangetout make a superb accompaniment.

Gratin dauphinois

'If Playboy *did centrefolds of
potatoes . . .'*
LOYD GROSSMAN

*2 lb (1 kg) firm waxy potatoes, peeled
and very thinly sliced
1 oz (25 g) butter
1-2 cloves garlic, crushed
1 tablespoon finely chopped fresh
parsley
Salt and freshly ground black pepper
10 fl oz (300 ml) single cream*

Layer the potatoes in a gratin dish
with dots of half the butter and the
garlic and parsley. Season each layer
with salt and freshly ground black
pepper. Pour over the cream and dot
the remaining butter on top. Bake at
gas mark 3, 325°F (160°C), for 1½
hours.

Sauce hollandaise

Hollandaise sauce always seems
difficult to a beginner but I find that
the more you make it, the easier it
becomes. It hardly takes me any
time to make now, so have patience
with it. However, it doesn't take
kindly to being kept waiting around,
so make it at the last minute.

*3 egg yolks
A pinch of salt
½ teaspoon caster sugar
2 tablespoons lemon juice
1 tablespoon white wine vinegar
6 oz (175 g) butter*

Put the egg yolks, salt and sugar in a
blender or food processor and give a
quick whiz to mix. Heat the lemon
juice and vinegar in a small pan and
melt the butter in another. When the
lemon juice and vinegar are almost
boiling, take off the heat and very
very slowly pour the mixture into the
blender with the motor running.
When that is incorporated, do exactly
the same with the butter, pouring it in
a very thin stream. (If the butter is
added too quickly, the sauce will
curdle.)

Crêpe soufflé on raspberry coulis

FOR THE CRÊPES
4 oz (100 g) plain white flour
5 fl oz (150 ml) milk
3 fl oz (85 ml) water
2 eggs
1 oz (25 g) butter

FOR THE FILLING AND COULIS
2 egg whites
2 tablespoons caster sugar
4 teaspoons lemon juice
2 firm kiwi fruits, peeled and sliced
8–10 oz (225-275 g) fresh or frozen
raspberries, thawed if frozen
A few fresh mint leaves, to decorate

Make the crêpes by putting the flour, milk, water and eggs in a blender or food processor. Whiz until smooth. Melt the butter in a small crêpe or omelette pan and swirl around the base, tipping any excess out into a jug. When the pan is quite hot and begins to smoke, pour in a small amount of the batter and swirl round to cover the bottom of the pan. When cooked on one side, slide a spatula underneath, flip over and cook on the other side. These crêpes have to be a little thicker than the normal pancake. Make 3 more crêpes, stacking them on a plate with greaseproof paper in between. Leave to cool.

When you are ready to make the dessert, whip up the egg whites until they form stiff peaks (as for meringue), then fold in the caster sugar with a metal spoon. The lemon juice can go in either with the sugar or after it. Place a good 2 teaspoonfuls of the mixture on one half of each crêpe, and a few slices of kiwi fruit, fold over and transfer to a well-buttered baking tray. Bake at gas mark 5, 375°F (190°C), for 3–5 minutes.

To make the coulis, sieve the raspberries into a small pan, reserving a few whole ones for decoration. Heat the coulis gently.

To serve, put a crêpe on each plate and surround with the raspberry coulis. Decorate with whole raspberries and mint leaves. Serve immediately.

PETER SAYERS'S MENU

·
STARTER
Avocado pear with a redcurrant dressing

·
MAIN COURSE
Monkfish in a blanket

·
DESSERT
Upside-down apple pecan pie

Avocado pear with a redcurrant dressing

3 egg yolks
Sea salt and black pepper
½ teaspoon French mustard
10 fl oz (300 ml) olive or walnut oil, tepid
1 tablespoon white wine vinegar, tepid
4 oz (100 g) redcurrants or blackcurrants
A few drops of balsamic vinegar (optional)
2 avocados
Lemon juice

Whisk, blend or process the egg yolks, salt, pepper and mustard together until thoroughly blended. Add the tepid oil a drop at a time, continuing to whisk or blend, and increasing the flow to a steady thin stream as the mayonnaise thickens. When all the oil has been incorporated, whisk or blend in the tepid vinegar to thicken slightly. If using a blender or food processor, add the currants, and a few drops of balsamic vinegar if you wish. Blend or process, and sieve before use. If making the dressing by hand, sieve the currants before adding them to the mayonnaise. Whisk in the balsamic vinegar if using and mix well.

Halve, stone and peel the avocados and coat all over with lemon juice to prevent browning. Slice each half avocado upwards from the thick end and spread out like a fan. Divide the mayonnaise between 4 plates and arrange the sliced avocados on top.

Monkfish in a blanket

'A very nice, light, fresh taste.'
SOPHIE GRIGSON

1 × 1½–2 lb (750 g–1 kg) monkfish
tail
2 oz (50 g) black olives, stoned
7 tablespoons olive oil
A few drops of balsamic or white wine
vinegar
4 oz (100 g) ground almonds
1 lb (450 g) courgettes
2 teaspoons salt
2 heaped teaspoons chopped fresh or 1
heaped teaspoon dried thyme
Black pepper
3 tablespoons chopped fresh or 2
tablespoons dried mint

Clean, trim and dry the fish, and make several diagonal incisions along the top. Blend or process the olives, 2 teaspoons olive oil and the vinegar together, or pound in a mortar and pestle, to make a paste. Mix 1 oz (25 g) olive paste with 1 oz (25 g) ground almonds and rub into the surface of the fish, ensuring it gets into all the cuts. Cover and leave for at least 1 hour.

Meanwhile, coarsely grate the courgettes, reserving a quarter of 1 courgette for garnish. Mix the grated courgettes with the salt and place in a colander to drain for at least 30 minutes. Then rinse twice in cold, running water and squeeze to remove excess moisture. Mix in the remaining ground almonds and half the thyme and season with black pepper. Spread the courgette mixture evenly and firmly over the fish. Add the remaining thyme and drizzle 1–2 tablespoons olive oil over the topping.

Bake in a pre-heated oven at gas mark 7, 425°F (220°C), for 5 minutes. Reduce the heat to gas mark 5, 375°F (190°C), and cook for a further 35–40 minutes. Heat the remaining olive oil in a pan with the mint and leave to infuse. Sieve and reheat the minted oil and pour over the fish just before serving. Garnish with slices of courgette.

Upside-down apple pecan pie

*'Wonderfully wicked-sounding. I love
the multi-layering.'*
SOPHIE GRIGSON

*9 oz (250 g) wholemeal flour
2 oz (50 g) granulated sugar
2 oz (50 g) vegetable fat
3 oz (75 g) butter
1 tablespoon vegetable oil
2 oz (50 g) pecan nuts, shelled
2 oz (50 g) brown sugar
1 lb (450 g) dessert apples (preferably
Golden Delicious)
A good pinch of cinnamon*

Put 8 oz (225 g) flour and 1 oz (25 g) granulated sugar in a bowl. Cut the vegetable fat and 2 oz (50 g) butter into small pieces and rub into the flour and sugar until it resembles breadcrumbs. Add the oil and enough water to form a stiff mixture. Knead well, cover and refrigerate until required.

Chop the pecan nuts, leaving 6–8 whole ones for decoration. Heat the remaining 1 oz (25 g) butter in a pan until bubbling and add the brown sugar. Add the chopped nuts to the butter and sugar and cook for 1 minute. Spread the mixture over the base of a greased, lined, 8 in (20 cm) pie dish. Peel, core and thinly slice the apples. In a bowl, mix 1 oz (25 g) flour with 1 oz (25 g) granulated sugar and a good pinch of cinnamon. Mix the sliced apples thoroughly in this mixture.

Now roll out 2 rounds of pastry, one the size of the pie dish and the other 1 in (2.5 cm) larger. Place the larger round on top of the pecan nut mixture covering the base. Arrange the apple slices on top, layering to achieve a fairly level top. Cover with the second pastry round, sealing the edges with a little water. Turn or roll the pastry edge over to form a ring, which will help when the pie is inverted. Cut decorative shapes from any surplus pastry and bake separately.

Bake the pie at gas mark 5, 375°F (190°C), for 30–35 minutes until the pastry is brown and firm to the touch. Take it out of the oven and let it stand for a few minutes before inverting on to a serving dish. Decorate with the pastry shapes and whole pecans. Serve with fromage frais or Greek-style yoghurt.

The North-West

TONY FITZWILLIAM-PIPE'S MENU

·
STARTER
Baby squid stuffed with crab
·
MAIN COURSE
Chicken breasts with port and
orange mousse
Vegetable ramekins
·
DESSERT
Pistachio frais with plum coulis

Baby squid stuffed with crab

4 baby squid
1 salmon head
1 small whiting fillet
Bones of 1 lemon sole
1 small onion
1 leek
2 carrots
A sprig of fresh parsley
1 bouquet garni
1 large crab
2 tablespoons lemon juice
1–2 teaspoons freshly made garlic
purée (see p. 54)
4 tablespoons red vermouth
2 egg yolks
Salt and pepper
Black olives, to garnish

Clean the squid, reserving the tentacles and fins, and removing the quills. Place in a large pan the salmon head, whiting, lemon sole bones, onion, leek, carrots, parsley and bouquet garni. Add 3–4 pints (1.75–2.25 litres) water, bring to the boil and simmer for 30 minutes. Skim off any scum, then strain the stock through muslin and divide the resulting liquid evenly between 2 containers. You should have approximately 5 fl oz (150 ml) in each.

Clean the crab, extract both the white and brown meat and place in separate bowls. Reserve the crab legs for decoration. Chop the brown meat and mix in 1 tablespoon lemon juice, the chopped fins and tentacles from the squid and the garlic purée. Loosely stuff each squid with this mixture and secure the open end with a cocktail stick. Put the squid in an ovenproof dish with half the stock and bake at gas mark 5, 375°F (190°C), for 10 minutes.

Heat the vermouth in a pan with the remaining stock. Reduce to about 8 tablespoons until the liquid thickens and becomes slightly 'sticky'. Pour the sauce into a bowl and place over a pan of boiling water. Whisk in the egg yolks until thick and season lightly with salt and pepper. Roughly chop the white crabmeat, moisten with the remaining 1 tablespoon lemon juice and warm in the oven.

To serve, spoon some of the sauce on to each warmed plate. Put a squid in the centre and pile a quarter of the white crabmeat on one side. Decorate with the crab legs and black olives and serve immediately.

Chicken breasts with port and orange mousse

The balance is very important in this dish. Don't overdo the orange zest or the port because it's easy to mask the flavour of the chicken. Although it's time-consuming and a bit tedious it makes a difference if you force the chicken thigh meat through a sieve, rather than using a blender to get rid of all the stringy bits.

1 × 3 lb (1.5 kg) fresh chicken
1 onion
1 leek
2 carrots
1 bayleaf
1 bouquet garni
Salt and black pepper
2 egg whites
6 tablespoons smetana or soured cream
4 tablespoons port
Rind of 1 orange
1 small red pepper
1 tablespoon sugar

Remove the legs and wings from the chicken, then remove the 2 breast fillets. Separate the thigh joints from the drumsticks. Skin the breasts and thighs and set aside. Break up the chicken carcass and put this in a large pan with the wings and drumsticks. Add the onion, leek, carrots, bayleaf, bouquet garni and 1 pint (600 ml) water. Bring to the boil and simmer for 1½ hours. Skim off any scum, then strain the stock through muslin. Allow to cool and skim off any fat. Season very lightly with salt and black pepper.

Remove any fat, skin or sinew from the chicken thighs and cut the flesh off the bone. Roughly chop the flesh, place with the egg whites in a blender or food processor and blend until smooth. Pass through a fine sieve to remove any remaining skin or sinew. Add 2 tablespoons smetana or soured cream to the mousse, a little at a time, and stir in until it is all absorbed. Repeat this process with the port. Cut the orange rind into very fine strips, blanch in boiling water, then fold into the mousse.

Beat the chicken breasts flat, until they are about twice their original size. Put 2–3 tablespoons mousse in the centre of each breast. Then fold the edges upwards to form an envelope, enclosing the mousse, and secure with cocktail sticks. Wrap each stuffed breast loosely in foil and bake at gas mark 5, 375° F (190°C), for 20 minutes, or until the juices run clear.

Reduce the stock to approximately

4 tablespoons per portion, taste and adjust the seasoning. Allow the stock to cool slightly, then carefully beat in the remaining 4 tablespoons smetana or soured cream, a little at a time. Slowly bring the sauce back to the boil and reduce until slightly thickened.

For the garnish, cut 16 julienne strips of red pepper, and put 3 tablespoons water and the sugar in a small pan. Bring to the boil and add the strips of red pepper. Boil until virtually all the liquid has evaporated and the red pepper has caramelised.

To serve, divide the sauce between the 4 plates. Place 1 chicken breast on each plate and garnish with the caramelised strips of red pepper.

Vegetable ramekins

When you're blanching the courgettes all you have to do is cook them enough to make them bend – they become a soggy mess if you overcook them.

1 onion, chopped
4 medium carrots, chopped
A generous pinch of dried dill
Salt and pepper
2 medium parsnips, cored and chopped
1 teaspoon smetana or soured cream
3 oz (75 g) hazelnuts, skinned and chopped
2 courgettes, thinly sliced diagonally

Put the chopped onion and carrots in a small pan with a little water, add the dill and cover tightly. Cook gently until soft, then mash and season with salt and pepper. Put the parsnips in a small pan with a little water. Cover tightly, cook gently until soft, then mash with the smetana or soured cream, and season with salt and pepper. Add the skinned chopped hazelnuts. Blanch the sliced courgettes in boiling salted water, then refresh in cold water.

To assemble, lightly oil 4 ramekins and line them with courgette strips. Half fill each one with the parsnip and hazelnut mixture. Top with the carrot and onion mixture. Reheat just before serving.

Pistachio frais with plum coulis

This was something that I invented for the *MasterChef* competition. It's a good dessert if you want to avoid fatty food but you want to eat something special. Excellent for dieters!

5 tablespoons fromage frais
4 tablespoons Amaretto liqueur
5 tablespoons natural yoghurt
2 tablespoons clear honey
¾ × 0.4 oz (11 g) sachet powdered gelatine, dissolved in water as per instructions on sachet
3 oz (75 g) pistachio nuts, shelled and coarsely chopped
2 egg whites
2 oz (50 g) curd cheese
1–2 lb (450 g–1 kg) red plums
A few small fresh mint leaves, to decorate
A few whole pistachio nuts, to decorate

Mix together the fromage frais, Amaretto, yoghurt and honey in a bowl. Add the dissolved gelatine, then fold in the pistachio nuts. Beat the egg whites until stiff and fold into the mixture. With a small teaspoon, make pea-sized balls of curd cheese and fold these into the mixture without breaking up the balls. Spoon the mixture into a mould and refrigerate until set.

To make the coulis, halve and stone the plums. Put them in a heavy-based saucepan with about 1 tablespoon water. Simmer for about 20 minutes or until the plums have become a pulp and most of the liquid has been reduced. Transfer to a blender or food processor and purée. Allow to cool.

To serve, turn out the fromage frais mixture in the centre of a plate. Spoon sufficient plum coulis on to the plate to surround the frais mixture. Decorate with small mint leaves and pistachio nuts.

CAROL ALEXANDER'S MENU

•

STARTER
Fish plaits with spinach and
watercress sauce

•

MAIN COURSE
Dambuster steak
Minted new potatoes
Vegetables julienne

•

DESSERT
Summer fruit brûlé

Fish plaits with spinach and watercress sauce

It's important to have small fillets
that are the same size, otherwise
they can be difficult to plait.

FOR THE SAUCE
Bones of 1 small turbot, brill or
Dover sole
1 thick slice of onion
1 carrot
1 stick celery
A few fresh parsley stalks
1 bayleaf
A good pinch of dried thyme or a sprig
of fresh thyme
A few white peppercorns
A little white wine
4 oz (100 g) spinach
½ bunch watercress
¾ oz (20 g) butter
1 tablespoon flour
2 fl oz (50 ml) single cream
1 tablespoon chopped fresh parsley
Salt and pepper

FOR THE FISH PLAITS
1 small turbot, brill or Dover sole,
filleted
2 fillets pink-fleshed trout
Oil, to grill
A little melted butter
Salt and pepper

For the sauce, first make the fish
stock. Put the fish bones, onion,
carrot, celery stick, parsley stalks,
bayleaf, thyme and white peppercorns in a pan and cover with water.

Bring to the boil, simmer for 20 minutes and strain. Return to the pan and boil until reduced by half for a stronger flavour. Then add enough white wine to make 5 fl oz (150 ml).

Cook the spinach briefly in boiling water for about 5 minutes. Throw the watercress leaves into the boiling water and cook for 4 minutes. Drain well. Put the spinach and watercress in a food processor and chop up finely. Melt the butter in a small pan over a low heat. Stir in the flour and cook together for 1 minute, stirring all the time. Pour in the strained stock and wine and stir until blended. Add the cream and simmer for 3 minutes, still stirring. Allow the sauce to cool slightly, then put it in a blender or food processor with the spinach, watercress and chopped parsley. Blend or process until the sauce is smooth and green. Return it to a clean pan and reheat, adding salt and pepper to taste.

Cut the fish into thin equal strips to make 8 strips of white fish and 4 of pink. Take 2 strips of white fish and 1 of pink, and carefully plait them. Repeat to make 4 plaits. Brush the grill rack lightly with oil. Pre-heat the grill. Then place the plaits on the grill rack, brush with melted butter, season, and grill, topside only, for approximately 5 minutes or until cooked.

To serve, flood each plate with green sauce and carefully place a fish plait on top.

Dambuster steak

I love to bring old English recipes up to date and this is based on a very traditional English dish of course. Remember, the secret of Yorkshire puddings is to have the fat as hot as possible in the trays.

FOR THE STEAK
1 lb (450 g) rump steak
2 oz (50 g) butter
2 tablespoons olive oil
1 clove garlic, crushed
1 tablespoon flour
2 tablespoons brandy
¼–½ bottle red wine
5 fl oz (150 ml) strong beef stock
Salt and pepper
1 bouquet garni (made with fresh parsley, thyme and 1 bayleaf)
4 oz (100 g) button mushrooms
½ small tin smoked mussels, drained

FOR THE YORKSHIRE PUDDINGS
4 oz (100 g) plain white flour
A pinch of salt
2 eggs
About 5 fl oz (150 ml) milk (more may be needed)
1 tablespoon oil

Cut the beef into 1 in (2.5 cm) cubes and melt 1½ oz (40 g) butter with the oil in a large pan. Brown the beef, add the crushed garlic, sprinkle on the flour and stir until thoroughly hot. Sprinkle on the brandy and ignite. Add 5 fl oz (150 ml) wine and the stock and bring to the boil. Season lightly with salt and pepper, and add the bouquet garni. Cover and simmer for 1½ hours, adding more wine if necessary. After this time the sauce should be sufficiently reduced.

To make the Yorkshire puddings, sift the flour and salt together in a bowl. Make a well in the centre, break in the eggs and add half the milk. Stir well, then add the remaining milk, beating vigorously (a balloon whisk is best for this). The batter should be the consistency of double cream: add a little more milk if needed. Leave to stand for 1 hour. Pre-heat the oven to gas mark 7, 425°F (220°C), about 15–20 minutes before it's required. Heat the oil in the Yorkshire pudding tins until very hot, pour in the batter and cook for 15–20 minutes, until golden brown and well risen.

Cook the mushrooms in the remaining ½ oz (15 g) butter in a frying pan for 2 minutes. Add to the steak, along with the smoked mussels, and continue cooking for another 10 minutes. Fill each Yorkshire pudding with steak, mushrooms and mussels, and serve. Accompany with minted new potatoes and lightly cooked julienne vegetables.

Summer fruit brûlé

You can use frozen or fresh fruit and vary the liqueur according to taste. This makes an excellent last-minute dessert. If you stand the dishes under the grill in a baking tray with ice, it stops the cream melting and allows you to get a more intense heat on the top.

1 lb (450 g) fresh or frozen summer fruits (e.g. redcurrants, blackcurrants, raspberries and blackberries), thawed if frozen
2 tablespoons kirsberry liqueur or any fruit liqueur
Rind and juice of 1 small orange
1 teaspoon arrowroot or cornflour
5 fl oz (150 ml) double cream
5 fl oz (150 ml) natural yoghurt
2 oz (50 g) dark soft brown sugar
2 oz (50 g) caster sugar

Put the summer fruit in a bowl, pour over the liqueur and leave to stand. Blanch the orange rind in boiling water for a few minutes, drain and reserve. Mix the orange juice with the arrowroot or cornflour, then strain the juice from the summer fruit and add to the arrowroot paste. Bring to the boil to thicken, and allow to cool.

Divide the fruit between 4 individual heatproof dishes and pour over the thickened juice. Whip the cream to a thick floppy consistency. Stir the yoghurt in the pot, then fold into the cream. Snip the reserved orange rind over the cream, then fold in. Spread the cream mixture over the fruit in the small dishes and refrigerate.

Combine the sugars together and spread evenly over the cream. Heat the grill to very hot and place the dishes underneath. Caramelise the sugar for a few minutes, then refrigerate to cool. Tap the caramel with a spoon to break it up when ready to eat.

RACHEL RUTTER'S MENU

·

STARTER

Smoked salmon mousse with tomato coulis

·

MAIN COURSE

Filet mignon of pork with leeks in cider
Spicy apple conserve
Potato nests
Glazed carrots and roast parsnips

·

DESSERT

Pears poached in port with cinnamon shortbread and chantilly cream

Smoked salmon mousse with tomato coulis

This is quite rich so you don't want too much of it. It's delicious served at a summer buffet to accompany cold meats and salads. Make sure that the mixture isn't too cold when adding the gelatine.

½ onion
½ carrot
1 bayleaf
10 black peppercorns
5 fl oz (150 ml) milk
1½ teaspoons powdered gelatine
1 × 6 oz (175 g) salmon steak
1 tablespoon red wine
1 tablespoon red wine vinegar
Juice of 1½ lemons
A sprig of fresh tarragon
A sprig of fresh lemon balm
A pinch of salt
½ oz (15 g) butter
1 tablespoon plain white flour
4 small thin slices smoked salmon
2 tablespoons natural yoghurt
1 egg white
Pepper
*1 × 2 in (5 cm) piece cucumber, thinly
diced*
*1 lb (450 g) tomatoes, roughly
chopped*
*2 teaspoons chopped fresh herbs
(including thyme, tarragon, chives and
lemon balm)*
A pinch of sugar
2 teaspoons sesame oil

Put the onion, carrot, bayleaf and 6 peppercorns in a pan with the milk. Bring to the boil and leave to infuse for about 30 minutes. In a bowl placed over hot water, put 2 tablespoons water and the gelatine and allow to dissolve. Place the salmon steak on a large square of foil. Sprinkle over the red wine, red wine vinegar, juice of ½ lemon, sprigs of tarragon and lemon balm, 4

peppercorns and a pinch of salt. Fold in the edges of the foil to enclose the steak completely and bake at gas mark 4, 350° F (180° C), for about 30 minutes until the flesh is set. Leave to cool in the foil.

Strain the flavoured milk into a clean pan. Stir in the butter and flour and whisk over a gentle heat until the butter has melted. Increase the heat and stir until thick. Allow to cool. Flake the warm salmon into a blender or food processor, add the smoked salmon, cooled sauce, juice of ½ lemon and the yoghurt. Blend until completely smooth. While the mixture is still a little warm, add the gelatine mixture and blend again for a few seconds. Whisk the egg white in a clean, grease-free bowl until it stands up in peaks. Turn the salmon mixture into the bowl, fold in gently and season with pepper. Oil 4 small fish moulds and spread a little of the mixture in each mould. Fold the diced cucumber into the remaining mousse mixture and continue to fill the moulds. Refrigerate until set.

To make the coulis, simmer the tomatoes with the juice of ½ lemon, the chopped fresh herbs and the sugar until soft and pulpy. Sieve into a clean bowl and stir in the oil. To serve, pour a little tomato coulis on to each plate and turn out a salmon mousse in the centre. Garnish with a tiny sliver of smoked salmon, or tiny pieces of the herbs used in the coulis.

Filet mignon of pork with leeks in cider

This is a family favourite. The sauce is easy to do but make sure it's reduced well. It's the sort of dish which won't come to any harm if your guests are late. Just leave it in a barely warm oven and it will be fine.

1½ lb (750 g) pork tenderloin fillets
1 tablespoon grapeseed oil
1 onion, chopped
½ bottle cider
4 small leeks, sliced
Salt and pepper
4 teaspoons finely chopped fresh lemon balm
8 fl oz (250 ml) double cream
A few sprigs of fresh lemon balm, to garnish
Chopped fresh chives, to garnish

Slice the pork diagonally across the grain in 8 thin or 4 thick slices. Beat the slices between clingfilm to flatten and tenderise the meat. Heat the oil in a pan and quickly seal the meat. Transfer 2 thin slices or 1 thick slice to each of 4 squares of foil. Add the onion to the pan and cook gently to soften (this makes the onion more digestible), add the cider and boil for a couple of minutes. Spread the sliced leeks over the meat, pour over the onion and cider, season with salt and pepper and top with chopped lemon balm. Fold up each foil square to enclose the meat and bake at gas mark 4, 350°F (180°C), for about 1 hour. Because the meat has so little fat it benefits from slower cooking in juices to prevent it from drying out.

To serve, transfer the contents of the parcels to a warm dish and tip the juices into a pan. Cover the meat and leeks with foil while preparing the sauce. Taste and adjust the seasoning of the juices, then boil to reduce and concentrate the flavours. Stir in the cream and heat but do not boil. Pour over the meat and garnish with tiny sprigs of lemon balm and chopped chives.

Spicy apple conserve

The Elizabethans made a lot of preserves and used to boil them for different lengths of time depending on how the preserves were to be used. The same recipe could be boiled for a short time to make a sauce, boiled longer to give the consistency of a modern-day jam, or boiled until really thick to be cut into shapes and stored as lozenges to decorate the table with jewelled colours when fresh foods became unobtainable. This conserve can be prepared in a similar way. Boiled up and bottled as a sauce, it will keep just like any preserve and can then be gently re-simmered to give a lovely rosy, spicy preserve ideal for serving with meats.

2 lb (1 kg) cooking apples, roughly chopped (including the peel and cores)
2 in (2.5 cm) piece fresh ginger, peeled and chopped
1 in (2.5 cm) cinnamon stick
A few blades of mace
Grated rind and juice of 2 lemons
About 2¾ lb (1.25 kg) sugar
2 lb (1 kg) Cox's Orange Pippin apples, peeled, cored and sliced
2 tablespoons brandy

Put the cooking apples in a pan with 2 pints (1.2 litres) water, the spices and lemon rind. Bring to the boil and simmer for about 1 hour until soft. Sieve into a clean pan and add the lemon juice, and 1 lb (450 g) sugar to each 1 lb (450 g) sieved apple pulp. Heat gently to dissolve the sugar, then bring to the boil and simmer for 5 minutes. Add the sliced eating apples and simmer for 10–15 minutes until tender. Remove from the heat before the apple slices start to break up and stir in the brandy.

Pot into sterilised jars (washed and placed in a moderate oven for 5 minutes). Seal with circles of waxed paper or quickly screw on non-metallic tops while the preserve is piping hot. Store and reheat as needed. Either serve as an apple sauce or simmer very gently for an hour to give a lovely rosy-coloured thicker preserve.

Potato nests

'Like crisps for billionaires.'
LOYD GROSSMAN

4 large potatoes
Oil, to deep-fry

Peel and thinly slice the potatoes. Do not rinse, as the starch in the potatoes is needed to hold the nests together. Place a layer of slices in a wire basket. Put another smaller wire basket inside to hold the potato slices in a nest shape. Heat the oil until it bubbles, then deep-fry the potatoes until crisp and golden. Carefully remove from the baskets and fry for a few seconds longer. Keep warm until ready to serve.

Glazed carrots and roast parsnips

12 oz (350 g) carrots or baby carrots
1 oz (25 g) butter
1 tablespoon sugar
1 lb (450 g) parsnips
Sunflower oil, to roast
Salt and pepper

Peel the carrots if they are old, alternatively just scrub off any dirt. Baby carrots can be cooked whole. If they are too large cut them into even-sized pieces, and trim into long barrel shapes. Heat the butter and sugar together in a pan, add the carrots and just enough water to cover. Boil until the liquid has almost boiled away. If the carrots are not quite tender enough, add a little more water and continue boiling but don't over-boil. Peel the parsnips and cut them in a similar way to the carrots. Parboil in salted water for 10 minutes, then roast them in hot oil at gas mark 6, 400°F (200°C), for 30 minutes until crisp. Season the carrots and parsnips with a little salt and pepper and serve.

Pears poached in port with cinnamon shortbread and chantilly cream

I ate out in a restaurant a while ago and had pear sablé. It was dreadful and I decided I could do better so I came home and made up this recipe. I like to use home-made crystallised violets and you need to grow your own so as not to pick wild varieties. I find both the white and purple easy to cultivate. Simply brush the dry flowers with egg white and sprinkle with caster sugar. To crystallise angelica stems, blanch tender young stems in boiling water, de-string if necessary, then boil in a sugar syrup. Add more sugar and boil again each day until you have a saturated solution. Stand for a couple of days to allow the stems to absorb the sugar. Then dip them in boiling water, quickly drain and dip into caster sugar. Dry, then store.
The flavour is gorgeous, much better than those hard, tasteless, green stems you can buy.

FOR THE PEARS
8 oz (225 g) caster sugar
10 fl oz (300 ml) red wine
Juice of ½ lemon
1 in (2.5 cm) cinnamon stick
2 large pears
2 tablespoons port

FOR THE SHORTBREAD
4 oz (100 g) butter
2 oz (50 g) caster sugar
6 oz (175 g) plain white flour, sifted
1 teaspoon ground cinnamon

FOR THE CREAM
5 fl oz (150 ml) double cream
½ oz (15 g) vanilla-flavoured caster
sugar (see method), or to taste
Crystallised violets and angelica, to
decorate

For the pears, first prepare a sugar syrup by dissolving the caster sugar in 1 pint (600 ml) water. Stir over a gentle heat until all the grains have dissolved, then bring to the boil. Stir in the red wine, lemon juice and cinnamon stick and leave to simmer while you prepare the pears. Peel the pears thinly. Halve each one and scoop out the core with a teaspoon. Poach the halves in the gently trembling liquid until tender, then allow to go cold in the syrup. Stir in the port just before you take them off the heat. (Adding liqueurs to poaching syrups at the end of the cooking time gives a better flavour.)

To make the shortbread, soften the butter in a bowl. (Only butter can give shortbread its traditional rich flavour.) Stir in the caster sugar and sifted flour. When mixed, stir in the ground cinnamon. Knead lightly and turn on to a lightly floured board. Roll out to about ¼ in (5 mm) thick and cut out rounds and crescents using a 3 in (7.5 cm) fluted scone cutter. Place on a floured baking sheet and bake at gas mark 5, 375°F (190°C), for 10–15 minutes until firm and pale gold. Allow to cool on a cooling tray. If the biscuits are to be stored put them in an airtight tin as soon as they are completely cold.

To make the chantilly cream, whisk the double cream with the vanilla-flavoured caster sugar (this is made by storing a vanilla pod in a large screw-topped jar filled with caster sugar, and shaking occasionally to distribute the flavour). When stiff, place in an icing bag fitted with a large rosette nozzle.

To assemble, pipe a large swirl of cream on to each shortbread round. Slice the cold, drained pear halves into fans and place a fan on each shortbread biscuit. Top with a rosette of cream and a crescent of shortbread. Decorate with home-made crystallised violets and angelica.

119

Scotland and the North-East

JOAN BUNTING'S MENU

STARTER
Goat's cheese and cherry parcels

MAIN COURSE
Guineafowl with Pineau des Charentes
Rice timbales
Carrot and courgette ribbons
Broccoli with pine nuts

DESSERT
Parfait Dentelles

Goat's cheese and cherry parcels

Be careful about the goat's cheese you use – if it's too hard, it won't melt enough; too soft and it will melt away completely.

4 small round English goat's cheeses
4 teaspoons Kirsch
4 sheets filo pastry
About 4 tablespoons melted unsalted butter
8 teaspoons Morello cherries (in their juice)
4 teaspoons sesame seeds
4 tablespoons grapeseed oil
1 tablespoon cherry juice
A squeeze of lime juice
Salt and pepper
Mixed salad leaves

De-rind the goat's cheeses, sprinkle each one with 1 teaspoon Kirsch and set aside for at least 1 hour. Take 1 sheet of filo and brush with melted butter. Fold in half and cut out as large a circle as possible. Brush with butter. Place a goat's cheese in the centre of the filo and put about 2 teaspoons cherries on top of the cheese. (Reserve a few cherries for decoration.) Gather the filo pastry over the cherries and pinch together to form a parcel. Brush with butter and scatter over 1 teaspoon sesame seeds.

120

Repeat with the other ingredients to make 4 parcels in total.

Place the parcels on a greased baking tray and bake at gas mark 6, 400°F (200°C), for 10–15 minutes until golden. Meanwhile, put the oil, cherry juice, lime juice and salt and pepper in a screwtop jar with a tight-fitting lid. Shake well and use to dress the salad leaves. Serve the parcels very hot on individual plates with the dressed salad. Garnish with the reserved cherries.

Guineafowl with Pineau des Charentes

Do try to get fresh not frozen guineafowl. Pineau des Charentes is a mixture of Cognac and unfermented grape juice which you can get in most large supermarkets. I find it very useful for cooking all sorts of fowl.

'Guineafowl . . . a chicken with a good CV.'

LOYD GROSSMAN

1 tablespoon melted butter
1 tablespoon olive oil
2 tablespoons chopped salt pork or unsmoked bacon
2 guineafowl
5 fl oz (150 ml) Pineau des Charentes
5 fl oz (150 ml) chicken stock
Salt and pepper
4 kumquats, sliced, or orange slices, to garnish
½ oz (15 g) butter
½ (15 g) sugar

Heat the butter and oil in a large casserole dish. Fry the salt pork or bacon until golden. Add the guineafowl and brown carefully on all sides. Add the Pineau, cover and cook until tender. Remove the guineafowl and carve, removing the breasts, legs and thighs. Keep warm. Add the stock to the casserole and reduce to a rich sauce. Season with salt and pepper, then strain. Briefly sauté the kumquats or orange slices in the butter and sugar. On each plate, arrange a portion of breast and leg with some sauce, and garnish with the sliced kumquats or orange slices.

Rice timbales

A good pinch of saffron strands
2 oz (50 g) butter
2–3 shallots, chopped
2 oz (50 g) long-grain rice (dry
weight), cooked
Salt and pepper
2 oz (50 g) wild rice (dry weight),
well cooked
2 teaspoons finely chopped fresh parsley

Put the saffron strands in a bowl with 2 tablespoons boiling water and leave to infuse. Thoroughly butter 4 moulds or ramekins. Melt half the remaining butter in a pan and soften half the chopped shallots. Stir in the white rice. When warmed, add the strained saffron liquid, reserving 4 softened strands to decorate, and season with salt and pepper. Half-fill each mould, pressing the rice in firmly. Repeat with the wild rice, using the remaining butter and shallots, and adding parsley instead of saffron. Season, fill the moulds and cover each one with buttered foil. Keep warm. To serve, unmould and decorate with a strand of saffron.

Carrot and courgette ribbons

Any wholegrain mustard will do, if you can't get hold of raspberry. Ideally use any fruit-flavoured or honey-flavoured variety.

4 medium carrots
4 medium courgettes
½ oz (15 g) butter
Salt and pepper
1 teaspoon raspberry or other
wholegrain mustard

Cut the carrots and courgettes into ribbons using a potato peeler. Steam until just tender. Melt the butter in a pan and season with salt, pepper and mustard. Dress the vegetables with the seasoned butter and serve.

Broccoli with pine nuts

1 small handful broccoli spears,
trimmed
1 oz (25 g) butter
Walnut or hazelnut oil
2 teaspoons pine nuts
Salt and pepper

Blanch the broccoli briefly in boiling salted water and drain. Melt the butter in a frying pan or wok. Add an equal quantity of oil and sauté the pine nuts until golden. Remove and drain. Stir-fry the broccoli until crisp but tender, season, and garnish with the pine nuts.

Parfait Dentelles

I named this dessert after the Dentelle mountains where the Beaumes de Venise Vineyards are: one of my favourite places in France. Fresh apricots or peaches work extremely well when they are in season, instead of mango.

2 eggs, separated
6 oz (175 g) caster sugar
10 fl oz (300 ml) double cream
4 tablespoons Muscat de Beaumes de Venise
1 oz (25 g) ground almonds
1 large, very ripe mango
2 oz (50 g) good-quality plain chocolate

Beat the egg yolks with 2 oz (50 g) caster sugar until pale and fluffy. Beat the cream until stiff, then fold into the egg yolk mixture. Add 2 tablespoons Muscat and divide the mixture between 4 parfait moulds. Freeze until solid.

Meanwhile, beat the egg whites until they stand up in peaks. Add the remaining 4 oz (100 g) caster sugar and the ground almonds. Pipe or spoon the meringue mixture into the same shape as the parfait moulds, making 4 meringues. Then place in the bottom of the oven at gas mark 2, 300°F (150°C), for 1½ hours.

Peel the mango, reserving 8 slices for decoration. Blend or process the remainder with the remaining 2 tablespoons Muscat, or to taste.

Remove the meringues from the oven and allow to cool. Melt the chocolate in a bowl over hot water, then spoon into an icing-cone made from greaseproof paper with a small hole cut in the end.

Pipe a thin line of chocolate in the desired shape on each cold plate. Flood the chocolate outline (e.g. a heart shape) with mango purée. Turn out the parfaits and decorate the sides with melted chocolate. Place a meringue shape on top of each parfait, and 2 slices of mango, and serve.

MARY OSWELL'S MENU

•
STARTER
Stir-fried prawns with ginger, green peppercorns, lemon and cucumber
•
MAIN COURSE
Malaysian-style crispy chicken with three seasonings
Yellow rice (Nasi Kunyit)
Phoenix tail salad
•
DESSERT
Lime water ice with Kuih roses

Stir-fried prawns with ginger, green peppercorns, lemon and cucumber

Try to get frozen raw prawns for this rather than cooked ones
– they are obtainable from Chinese supermarkets.

1 lb (450 g) frozen raw prawns in their shells, thawed
A dash of white wine vinegar
A few black peppercorns
A pinch of salt
1 in (2.5 cm) piece fresh ginger
12 green peppercorns
½ cucumber
2 lemons
2 tablespoons very dry Sherry or Montilla
1 teaspoon arrowroot
1 teaspoon sesame oil
1 teaspoon light soy sauce
½ teaspoon sugar
1 tablespoon sunflower oil

Peel the prawns and put the heads and shells in a small pan for the stock. Cover with water, add the vinegar, black peppercorns and salt, and bring to the boil. Simmer for 30 minutes, skimming off any scum that forms. Strain and reserve.

Now cut the ginger into tiny matchsticks, lightly crush the green peppercorns and slice the cucumber into half moons, removing seeds as you go but not the rind. Peel the lemons, removing all white pith, and use a sharp knife to cut out the segments from between the membranes.

Put the Sherry or Montilla in a small bowl. Mix in the arrowroot, sesame oil, soy sauce and sugar, stirring well. Heat the sunflower oil in a wok or large frying pan over a medium heat. Cook the ginger matchsticks, add about 5 fl oz (150 ml) prawn stock and the arrowroot mixture. Cook for 1 minute until thick and glossy. Then add the prawns, cucumber matchsticks and lemon segments, and quickly stir-fry.

Malaysian-style crispy chicken with three seasonings

Make sure the chicken is very cold before it is bathed in boiling water, and put it straight back in the fridge afterwards.

2 in (5 cm) cinnamon stick
2 star anise pods
1 lime, cut in quarters
1 tablespoon honey
2 lb (1 kg) chicken joints (preferably wings)
Salt
Oil, to deep-fry

FOR THE SEASONINGS
1 tablespoon hoisin sauce
1 tablespoon Chinese plum sauce
1 teaspoon sesame oil
Sweet black rice vinegar, to taste
Allspice, to taste
Schechuan pepper, to taste
Lemon grass, to taste

Put the cinnamon stick, star anise pods, lime quarters and honey in a large pan. Half-fill the pan with water, bring to the boil and allow to infuse for a few minutes.

Place the chicken joints in a colander over a large saucepan and ladle the spiced water over them until the skin shrinks and turns translucent and glossy. (Wings work best because they are rather skinny, and the crispy skin is the best bit.) Quickly re-chill the joints so that they stay cold inside throughout. Refrigerate, uncovered, for about 5 hours.

When ready to cook, rub the joints with salt. Heat the oil until it bubbles and deep-fry the joints until crispy and well-cooked.

For the first seasoning, mix together the hoisin sauce and Chinese plum sauce. For the second, blend the sesame oil with the sweet black rice vinegar to taste. For the third seasoning, add together Schechuan pepper, lemon grass and allspice to taste.

Yellow rice (Nasi Kunyit)

8 oz (225 g) long-grain rice
A pinch of salt
A few black peppercorns
2 teaspoons ground turmeric
3 oz (75 g) creamed coconut

Put the rice in a large pan with 4 pints (2.25 litres) boiling water, the salt, peppercorns and turmeric. Boil quickly, uncovered, for 12–15 minutes until tender.

Meanwhile, make the coconut milk by dissolving the creamed coconut in 7 fl oz (200 ml) hot water. When the rice is cooked, drain it well, pour over the coconut milk and drain again. Put the rice in a dish, cover, and leave in a warm oven at gas mark 2, 300°F (150°C), until ready to serve.

Phoenix tail salad

FOR THE SALAD
4 oz (100 g) French beans
4 oz (100 g) mangetout
2 small carrots
1 small red pepper
2 cherry tomatoes
Watercress

FOR THE DRESSING
Juice of ½ lemon
2 tablespoons sunflower oil
¼ teaspoon salt
½ teaspoon caster sugar

Top and tail the French beans and mangetout. Blanch in boiling water and refresh in cold water. Slice the carrots and red pepper into thin strips. Put all the dressing ingredients in a screwtop jar with a tight-fitting lid. Shake well and pour over the salad. Arrange the salad ingredients in a fan shape so that the colours form a 'rainbow'.

Lime water ice with Kuih roses

FOR THE WATER ICE
Finely peeled green rind of 2 and juice
of 8 limes
10 oz (275 g) granulated sugar
2 fl oz (50 ml) gin

FOR THE KUIH ROSES
2 oz (50 g) plain white flour
2 oz (50 g) rice flour
2 oz (50 g) caster sugar
3 oz (75 g) creamed coconut
Oil, to deep-fry

To make the water ice finely peel 2 limes, avoiding all pith which is very bitter. Cut the peel into tiny matchsticks and boil for 10–15 minutes in 10 fl oz (300 ml) water, then drain, reserving the water. Dissolve 2–3 oz (50–75 g) sugar into the reserved water and boil to a syrup. Add the lime matchsticks and gin. Take off the heat and allow to cool, then add the lime juice. Pour into a polythene container and freeze, uncovered, until almost solid. Remove and whisk thoroughly. Freeze, covered, until ready to serve.

For the roses, put the plain flour, rice flour and caster sugar in a bowl. Dissolve the creamed coconut in 7 fl oz (200 ml) hot water, then beat into the flour and sugar to make a batter. Heat a pan of oil, then dip each mould in the hot oil. When hot, dip the mould into the batter, then quickly back into the oil. Shake the mould to release the rose and continue with the remaining batter until you have 12–16 roses. Skill increases with patience! Allow the roses to cool before serving.

Serve each person with a large scoop of lime water ice and 3–4 Kuih roses. A small glass of lime gin can accompany each serving or be poured over the water ice.

LILY GIBB'S MENU

·

STARTER
Arbroath smokie creel

·

MAIN COURSE
Medallions of venison

·

DESSERT
Pears-à-la-tay

Arbroath smokie creel

Arbroath smokies are wood-smoked haddock which this region is famous for. Most larger fish merchants should have them, but if they don't, you could use any sort of smoked fish. A creel is a wooden slatted basket that fishwives used to carry on their backs and I use a scallop shell to mould the pastry into a similar shape.

FOR THE PASTRY SHELLS
8 oz (225 g) plain white flour
A pinch of salt
4 oz (100 g) butter, diced
3 tablespoons ice-cold water

FOR THE FILLING
1 oz (25 g) butter
½ oz (15 g) plain white flour
5 fl oz (150 ml) chicken stock
Pepper
½ onion, finely chopped
2 oz (50 g) mushrooms, sliced
2 fl oz (50 ml) vermouth
A pinch of ground turmeric
A pinch of dried thyme
½ tablespoon lemon juice
A pinch of dried parsley
5 fl oz (150 ml) single cream
2 Arbroath smokies
Lemon slices and sprigs of fresh parsley, to garnish

To make the pastry, put the flour and salt in a bowl. Rub in the butter until the texture resembles breadcrumbs. Add the water and gently knead together to form a dough. Roll out on a floured board, then cut out 4 round shapes with a clean scallop shell. Press each pastry round into the scallop to mould it into a shell shape. Place on a baking sheet, put some scrunched-up foil in each shell so they keep their shape, and bake blind at gas mark 6, 400°F (200°C), for 12–15 minutes until lightly browned. Keep warm.

For the filling, begin by making a velouté sauce. Melt ½ oz (15 g) butter in a pan. Add the flour and cook for a few seconds, stirring. Mix in the chicken stock, stirring over the heat until the sauce thickens. Season with pepper and cook for several more minutes until the sauce is smooth and syrupy. Reserve.

In another pan, gently heat the remaining ½ oz (15 g) butter and sweat the onion, taking care not to let it brown. Add the mushrooms and cook for 2 minutes. Add the vermouth and reduce the liquid by half. Now add 7 fl oz (200 ml) velouté sauce, the turmeric, thyme, lemon juice and parsley. Cook for 10 minutes, then add the cream, taking care not to let it boil. Take the smokies off the bone, flake and add to the sauce. Simmer gently for 5 minutes and check the seasoning.

To serve, spoon the smokie mixture into the warmed pastry shells and garnish with lemon slices and sprigs of parsley.

Medallions of venison

This is another dish with a very Scottish feel to it. The medallions should be no thicker than ¾ in (2 cm). I use farmed venison which has a less strong flavour than wild and tends to appeal to more people.

'The sort of thing you'd eat before invading England.'
LOYD GROSSMAN

2 tablespoons oil
1 tablespoon finely diced carrot
1 tablespoon finely diced onion
½ stick celery, finely chopped
1 tablespoon plain white flour
15 fl oz (450 ml) beef consommé
10 fl oz (300 ml) red wine
1 tablespoon redcurrant jelly
4 × 6 oz (175 g) venison steaks, cut from the saddle
1 oz (25 g) butter
2 teaspoons juniper berries

Heat the oil in a pan, add the chopped vegetables and cook until barely coloured. Add the flour and cook slowly until the mixture is a russet-brown colour. Add the consommé and cook gently for 30–40 minutes. Skim well, strain, then return to the pan. Add the wine and redcurrant jelly and simmer until syrupy.

Wipe the venison steaks. Heat the butter in another pan and sauté the venison for 3½ minutes on each side. Once the medallions have been turned, add the juniper berries.

To serve, arrange the medallions on a hot dish and spoon over a little of the sauce. Serve the rest of the sauce separately. Accompany with new potatoes, baked tomatoes and courgettes or any vegetable in season.

Pears-à-la-tay

A tayberry is a cross between a raspberry and a loganberry, either of which would work well if you couldn't get hold of tayberries. This is an adaptation of a very old recipe which I remember seeing demonstrated at the Women's Rural Institute when I was a teenager. I usually serve it with home-made shortbread to give a crunchy texture. If the sauce is not sweet enough, add a little more sugar to the fruit when cooking, but it should be slightly tart.

8 oz (225 g) caster sugar
Juice of ½ lemon
4 pears
4 oz (100 g) tayberries
4 oz (100 g) blackcurrants
A few flaked almonds, toasted
5 fl oz (150 ml) pouring or
whipped cream

Put the sugar in a pan with 5 fl oz (150 ml) water. Bring to the boil and boil for 3 minutes. Take off the heat, add the lemon juice and allow to cool.

Peel the pears, halve them and remove the cores. Put the pear halves in the cooled sugar syrup and poach until tender. Then put them in 4 individual dishes or 1 large dish, allowing 1 pear per person. Meanwhile, put the tayberries and blackcurrants in a pan and place over a low heat. Add some of the syrup from the pears and simmer until all the juices have run out and the fruit is tender. Sieve the juice into a bowl and allow to cool.

To serve, spoon the cold fruit sauce over the pears and sprinkle with a few flaked almonds. Serve the cream separately.

The Home Counties

SILVIJA DAVIDSON'S MENU

.

STARTER

Rare poached wild salmon 'cakes'
with English asparagus

.

MAIN COURSE

Dry-spiced lamb
Stovied potatoes
Wilted spinach salad

.

DESSERT

Rose-scented rhubarb with creamy
yoghurt and pistachios

Rare poached wild salmon 'cakes' with English asparagus

This would be excellent for a picnic
or outdoor meal or even served as a
main course with salad. The tail-end
of the salmon, which is fine for this
dish, should come cheaper than the
middle 'steak' joint. A pronounced
V-shape in the tail is a sign of a
firm, vigorous and probably wild
fish. Cold-smoked halibut slices are
produced and packed in 1½ oz
(40 g) packets by Ogier of Norfolk.

*A generous handful of fresh tarragon
and/or chervil
1 fresh bayleaf
½ clove garlic
1 small shallot
2 in (5 cm) piece white of leek
6 black or white peppercorns
5 fl oz (150 ml) good-quality white
wine
2–3 teaspoons white wine vinegar
2 teaspoons sea salt
1 × 1 lb (450 g) tail-end wild salmon
1 lb (450 g) medium-thick asparagus
White pepper
A little grated horseradish or
½–1 teaspoon bottled horseradish
(not the sauce)
5 fl oz (150 ml) crème fraîche
1½ oz (40 g) cold-smoked halibut
2–4 sprigs fresh dill, finely chopped
Grapeseed or light olive oil
A few small fronds of fresh dill, to
garnish*

Select a pan large enough to hold the
salmon joint, and half-fill with cold
water. Add the herbs, garlic, shallot,
leek, peppercorns, wine, vinegar and
salt. Bring to the boil and simmer for a
few minutes before placing the
salmon in the liquid. Bring gently
back to the boil, then reduce the heat
immediately to give the barest simmer. Poach the salmon (which should
be covered by the liquid) for 2 minutes on one side, then turn carefully
and poach for a further 2 minutes.

Take the pan off the heat and cover. Leave the salmon to rest in the hot liquid for a further 20–30 minutes, depending on thickness. Remove the salmon and allow to cool.

Meanwhile, prepare the asparagus. Rinse well, and trim off any woody bits. Slice off the tips to about 1½ in (4 cm) length, and poach in lightly salted boiling water for 4–6 minutes, or until just tender. Remove, drain and reserve. Chop the remaining stalks roughly and poach in the same water until tender. (Reserve 3 tablespoons asparagus water if you wish, to use for Stovied potatoes, see page 134.) Remove, drain and purée the stalks in a food processor or blender, seasoning very lightly with salt and pepper. If the purée is very thick, dilute with a little cooking water until you have the consistency of a light sauce.

Stir the horseradish into the crème fraîche and season with salt and pepper. Slice the halibut into ¼ in (5 mm) strips. Skin and bone the salmon, separating the flesh into fairly large natural flakes. Mix gently with the strips of halibut, 2–3 teaspoons horseradish cream and the chopped sprigs of dill. Taste and adjust the seasoning, adding a few flakes of sea salt and a sprinkling of white pepper as needed. Lightly oil 4 ramekins or moulds and divide the salmon mixture between them, pressing down gently. Chill a little to set but aim to serve at room temperature.

When ready to serve, divide the asparagus purée and remaining horseradish cream between 4 small plates, swirling together roughly. Gently loosen the edges of the salmon moulds, then invert each one over the centre of the plate and shake gently to release. (If your courage fails, unmould the salmon first, then surround with sauce!) Arrange the asparagus tips (also tepid, not chilled) on the plates and garnish the salmon with a few fronds of dill.

Dry-spiced lamb

This recipe was developed for rare-breed lamb, which has a strong, 'dusky' flavour. Try to get well-hung meat, and omit honey if using new-season or spring lamb. When buying the lamb ask for the bones to use as stock for the potatoes. One whole eye of loin is sufficient for two servings: if using only one, fold back on itself when tying.

2 teaspoons light olive or grapeseed oil
2 × 10–12 oz (275–350 g) eyes of loin of lamb, trimmings reserved for stock
1 teaspoon ground cumin
1 teaspoon ground cinnamon
1 teaspoon ground coriander
Seeds from 4 cardamom pods, crushed
12 juniper berries, warmed and crushed
A pinch of allspice
A pinch of black pepper
2 teaspoons clear honey
1 scant teaspoon powdered mustard
¼ teaspoon Dijon mustard
1 teaspoon white poppy seeds
1 teaspoon sesame seeds
1 teaspoon pink peppercorns, lightly crushed (optional)

Massage the oil into the meat, then coat with the spices and berries and sprinkle with allspice and pepper. Wrap loosely in foil and refrigerate for 12–24 hours. Shortly before cooking, brush off the juniper berries and smear one side of each piece of meat with 1 teaspoon honey, half the powdered mustard and the Dijon mustard. Put the two pieces of meat together, honeyed sides facing each other, thick end to thin, and tie firmly but not too tightly at regular intervals. Coat with the remaining mustard, poppy and sesame seeds, using a little honey or oil to 'stick' the seeds if necessary. Pre-heat the oven to gas mark 8, 450°F (230°C).

When ready to cook the lamb, place on a rack in a suitable roasting dish and roast in the pre-heated oven for 12–15 minutes (press the meat to check for resilience and doneness or insert the tip of a thin-bladed knife and check pinkness). Remove from the oven and wrap in a double thickness of foil. Leave to rest in a warm place for 10–15 minutes before removing the string, slicing and serving.

Slice the meat carefully into medallions, sprinkle with pink peppercorns if wished and serve from a suitable warmed dish or arrange on plates with the potatoes and warm spinach salad.

Stovied potatoes

FOR THE STOCK
Lamb trimmings from the Dry-spiced
lamb (see p. 133)
1 teaspoon honey
A little Madeira (optional)
½ clove garlic
½ shallot
2 in (5 cm) piece white of leek
1 bayleaf
A sprig of fresh thyme
A sprig of fresh rosemary
A few allspice berries
2 black peppercorns
6 juniper berries

FOR THE POTATOES
1 lb (450 g) tiny new potatoes
(preferably Jersey Royals)
½ teaspoon sea salt
1 oz (25 g) unsalted butter
6 juniper berries (optional)

You can use stock or asparagus water to cook the potatoes. If you wish to use stock, first paint the bones and meat trimmings with the honey and place in a roasting dish in the oven at gas mark 9, 475°F (240°C), for about 20 minutes, until brown and caramelised.

Pour off the fat from the tin, then deglaze with a little water or Madeira, and pour this into a saucepan. Add the remaining stock ingredients, cover with cold water, bring to the boil and skim. Reduce the heat and simmer gently for a couple of hours or until ready to cook the potatoes.

Scrub the new potatoes and place them in a heavy-based saucepan with the salt, butter and either 6 table-spoons stock or 3 tablespoons aspara-gus water from the Rare poached wild salmon 'cakes' recipe (see p. 131), with the juniper berries if using. Cover and cook over a gentle heat for 10–15 minutes, depending on the size of the potatoes, or until tender, shaking the pan from time to time.

Once the potatoes are cooked, remove the lid, increase the heat, and drive off all excess liquid, shaking the pan vigorously, to leave each potato glossy. Transfer to a warm serving dish, discarding any juniper, or divide between the plates when serving the lamb.

Wilted spinach salad

12 oz (350 g) young spinach leaves,
washed and trimmed
A few young dandelion leaves or nettle
tops (optional)
1 small head red chicory and/or 8 red
radishes, thinly sliced
1½ oz (40 g) hazelnuts, toasted and
skinned
5 teaspoons light olive or grapeseed oil
1 tablespoon hazelnut oil
A few juniper berries (optional)
A pinch of black pepper
6 oz (175 g) oyster mushrooms
1 good teaspoon Dijon mustard
(preferably hazelnut-flavoured)
A pinch of sea salt
1 tablespoon medium-sweet Madeira
(preferably Bual)
2 teaspoons balsamic or wine vinegar

Warm a large serving or mixing bowl by rinsing in hot water, then dry thoroughly. Place the salad leaves, sliced chicory or radishes and toasted nuts in the bowl. Warm 3 teaspoons light olive or grapeseed oil with the hazelnut oil and infuse with the juniper berries if using. Discard the berries, mix the oil with the black pepper and use to toss the salad leaves.

Wipe the mushrooms if necessary, and slice roughly. Place in a non-stick pan with 2 teaspoons light olive or grapeseed oil, the mustard and salt. Stir thoroughly, cover and place over a medium heat until the juices begin to run. Remove the lid, increase the heat and drive off the liquid, stirring constantly. Add the Madeira and reduce once more until dry. Add the vinegar, stir around, remove from the heat and pour the mushroom mixture over the leaves and nuts. Toss thoroughly and serve warm from the bowl or on individual plates.

Rose-scented rhubarb with creamy yoghurt and pistachios

You must use a yoghurt without an acidic flavour for this. Although rose petal preserve is expensive it does make this dish special.

12 oz (350 g) slender pink rhubarb stems
4 tablespoons rose petal preserve
4–5 teaspoons rosewater
1 oz (25 g) caster sugar
1 oz (25 g) pistachio nuts, freshly shelled
2 small sticks angelica
1 × 8 oz (225 g) carton strained Greek yoghurt

Wash and trim the rhubarb, de-stringing if necessary. Cut into 1 in (2.5 cm) lengths, splitting the stems into batons if more than ½ in (1 cm) thick. Place in a heatproof bowl or heavy stainless steel pan with 3 table-spoons preserve and 2 teaspoons rosewater. Either bake at gas mark 4–5, 350–375°F (180–190°C), or simmer over the gentlest heat pos-sible, until just tender. Test after 20 minutes if baking, 10 minutes if sim-mering. Allow to cool, then refriger-ate.

Melt the caster sugar gently in a heavy-based pan. Add the pistachios and stir for 1 minute until glistening. Tip out on to greaseproof paper or an oiled plate, and separate whilst cooling. When cold, crush slightly with a rolling pin. Slice the angelica thinly and soak in 1–2 teaspoons warmed rosewater to dissolve off the sugar and gently flavour the angelica. Drain and set aside.

To serve, spoon the rhubarb com-pote into a glass or china serving dish, or 4 individual dishes. Blend 1 table-spoon preserve with 1 teaspoon rosewater and swirl lightly through the yoghurt, spooning this on top of the compote. Sprinkle with the pistachios and angelica.

ROBERT ASH'S MENU

.

STARTER

Red mullet fillets with samphire

.

MAIN COURSE

Boned best end neck of lamb with
Reform Club sauce
Ribboned vegetables

.

DESSERT

Tarte des demoiselles Tatin, avec
poires au vin rouge poivré

Red mullet fillets with samphire

I predict that samphire is going to
be the vegetable of the nineties. It's
so versatile and the tips are
excellent in salads for an extra
crunch and saltiness. The French
call mullet 'the woodcock of the sea'
because in both cases you don't
have to gut the animal: you can eat
it all. The disadvantage of red
mullet is that it's hard to fillet and
you may find yourself having to go
through it with a pair of tweezers to
remove the fine bones left behind.
You can use red snapper if you
prefer.

*8 red mullet fillets (bones, head, livers
and tails reserved for the stock)
5 fl oz (150 ml) dry white wine
2 cloves garlic, unpeeled
A small sprig of fresh thyme
1 oz (25 g) butter
8 oz (225 g) samphire
1 tablespoon olive oil
Salt
4 teaspoons lumpfish caviar
4 pimentos, finely chopped
4 black olives, stoned and finely
chopped*

First make a fish stock. Put the bones
and livers of the mullet in a pan with
the dry white wine, cover, bring to
the boil and simmer for 40 minutes.
This should give about 14 fl oz
(400 ml) liquid. Add the garlic and

thyme, uncover, increase the heat and reduce by half. Whisk in ½ oz (15 g) butter and pass the sauce through muslin or a fine sieve. Keep warm.

Wash the samphire, place in a pan and cover with boiling water. Boil for 4 minutes, then drain. Heat ½ oz (15 g) butter in the pan, return the drained samphire and stir thoroughly until glazed in the butter. Keep warm.

Heat the olive oil in a pan, lightly salt the fish fillets and fry them, skin-side down, until rose-coloured. Turn and cook on the other side.

To serve, run some sauce around each plate, then stir in 1 teaspoon caviar. Arrange 2 fillets on top of the sauce at one end, and a portion of samphire in the shape of a tree at the other. At the bottom of the 'tree', place a little chopped pimento and olive. Serve immediately.

Boned best end neck of lamb with Reform Club sauce

Don't be persuaded to use neck fillet which is just scrag end. You have to use a really good cut of meat.

A knob of unsalted butter
2 shallots, finely chopped
1 carrot, cut into julienne strips
1 slice good-quality smoked ham, cut into julienne strips
1 slice tongue, cut into julienne strips
3 tablespoons red wine vinegar or sherry vinegar
5 tablespoons port
5 fl oz (150 ml) lamb neck bone or chicken stock
1 clove
4 small blades mace
5 juniper berries
5 sprigs of fresh rosemary
1 teaspoon arrowroot
A little double cream
1 tablespoon chopped fresh coriander
A few pink peppercorns
1 tablespoon olive oil
4 fillets best end neck or loin of lamb

Heat the unsalted butter in a pan and fry the finely chopped shallots, carrot, smoked ham and tongue. Keep stirring, until just brown. Add the vinegar and port, and reduce until you have 2 tablespoons liquid. (Tilt the saucepan, holding back the solids, to measure.) Then add the stock, clove, mace, juniper berries and rosemary, and simmer for 30 minutes. Mix the arrowroot with a drop of water and stir into the sauce to thicken a little. Add some double cream, until you have a smooth consistency. Finally, add the chopped fresh coriander and pink peppercorns, and keep the sauce hot.

Just before serving, heat the olive oil in a large pan. Fry the lamb fillets for about 10 minutes on each side over a medium heat, turning them until well browned.

To serve, place a fillet on each plate, surround with some sauce and accompany with Ribboned vegetables.

Ribboned vegetables

2 courgettes
2 carrots
4 oz (100 g) mangetout
Salt

Using a mandolin or potato peeler, cut the courgettes and carrots into ribbons. Place in a steamer with the mangetout and cook over boiling water until tender, or cook in boiling salted water until just tender.

Tarte des demoiselles Tatin, avec poires au vin rouge poivré

I was taught to make Tarte Tatin the proper French way and this is a hybrid recipe incorporating poached pears in wine rather than whole apples. You can use a whole bottle of red wine and leave out the colouring to achieve a darker red colour if you wish. The pears need to marinate for 24 hours – 12 at a pinch. You also need a good cast iron saucepan that you can transfer from burner to oven. I serve this without an accompaniment although the French often serve crème fraîche (yoghurt is no substitute), and a thick crème anglaise would be beautiful with it. The bright yellow would look great against the red of the pears. This recipe serves six.

12 pears (preferably Comice, Anjou or Bosc)
Raspberry or wine vinegar
5 fl oz (150 ml) red wine
2 cinnamon sticks
2 cloves
4 black peppercorns
1 teaspoon scarlet food colouring (not cochineal)
7 oz (200 g) plain white flour
A pinch of salt
Sugar
3 egg yolks
½ teaspoon vanilla essence
5 oz (150 g) unsalted butter

Peel, core and halve the pears, then use a pastry brush to paint each half with vinegar to stop them discolouring. Place them in a large non-plastic bowl with the red wine, sticks of cinnamon, cloves, peppercorns, food colouring and enough water to cover the pears. Leave to marinate for 12–24 hours.

To make the *pâte sucrée*, sift the flour on to a clean board or marble slab. Make a well in the centre, and put in a pinch of salt, 3 oz (75 g) sugar, the egg yolks and the vanilla essence. Mix with the fingers until the sugar dissolves. Now work in 4 oz (100 g) unsalted butter from the centre. Bring in the flour from the edges, bit by bit, until you have a smooth dough. Then knead with the palm of your hand, until the dough comes away from the board without sticking. Sprinkle with flour and roll out the dough into a circle of 9–10 in (23–25 cm) in diameter. Place the dough in a plastic bag and refrigerate for 30 minutes.

Meanwhile, take a 9–10 in (23–25 cm) round cast iron pan (or one that can be used on the hob as well as inside the oven) and cover the base with sugar to a depth of ¼ in (5 mm). Arrange the pear halves on their sides in a spiral, each bulbous side touching the inside of the next pear. Put 2–3 pear halves in the centre. Dot 1 oz (25 g) butter in between the pears and place the pan over a medium heat. Do not move the pears, but keep turning the pan round to ensure even cooking. The butter and sugar will melt and start to caramelise. At this point lower the heat, as the boiling sugar will burn the pears very easily. Keep turning the pan for 10 minutes.

Meanwhile, pre-heat the oven to gas mark 5, 375°F (190°C). Take the pears off the heat and remove the pastry from the fridge. Lay the pastry over the pears, pressing down lightly, so that the pears fall 'domino' fashion on to their bulbous sides with the cut sides making a flat platform for the pastry.

Bake in the pre-heated oven for around 30 minutes, until the pastry is dark brown. Remove from the oven and leave the tart to stand for 10 minutes. Then place a metal tray several sizes larger than the pan face-down on to the pastry. Turn out, so that the pastry forms a base for the caramelised pears. Use a spoon to scoop up any juices and pour them over the pears.

JANET AITKEN'S MENU

·
STARTER
French onion soup with a croûton of Gruyère and garlic
·
MAIN COURSE
Wild pigeon breasts in a Cognac and mango sauce with wild mushrooms and herbs
Soft blue cheese potato gratin
Broccoli with garlic and fresh thyme steamed on a bed of glazed shallots
·
DESSERT
Tarte aux pommes with honey and almonds baked with a cheese crust and served with a chantilly cream

'The whole menu has a look of rustic France.'
LOYD GROSSMAN

French onion soup with a croûton of Gruyère and garlic

I had this soup in a little French restaurant in Chamonix on a skiing holiday. It came to the table boiling hot with a massive croûton which burned my tongue, but it tasted wonderful. Remember to put in plenty of garlic and ground black pepper and serve it piping hot.

2 oz (50 g) butter
2 lb (1 kg) onions, thinly sliced
1 teaspoon brown sugar
2½ pints (1.5 litres) pigeon, beef or lamb stock
5 fl oz (150 ml) dry white wine
4 tablespoons brandy
Salt and freshly ground black pepper
2 soft bread rolls, halved, or 1 small French stick, thickly sliced
6 oz (175 g) Gruyère cheese, thinly sliced
2 cloves garlic, crushed

Heat the butter in a large pan and fry the onions for 20 minutes or until very soft. Add the sugar and cook until the onions are golden brown. Add the stock and wine. Cover, bring to the boil and simmer for 1 hour. Add the brandy, and salt and freshly ground black pepper to taste.

Ten minutes before serving, toast the bread on one side, then place the sliced cheese on the other side and toast until bubbling and golden brown. Spoon on the crushed garlic, place the croûtons in the bowls and serve immediately.

Wild pigeon breasts in a Cognac and mango sauce with wild mushrooms and herbs

You must use the full cooking time. Never undercook pigeon as it gets more tender the longer you cook it. If you wish you can buy four whole pigeons, use the breasts and keep the carcasses for making the stock.

1½ oz (40 g) butter
2 medium onions, chopped
4 cloves garlic, sliced
8 pigeon breasts
1 ripe mango, peeled, stoned and chopped
8 oz (225 g) mushrooms, sliced
5 fl oz (150 ml) red wine
2 tablespoons honey
Juice of 1 lemon
Salt and freshly ground black pepper
10 fl oz (300 ml) pigeon, beef or lamb stock
3 tablespoons Cognac
1 tablespoon flour

Heat 1 oz (25 g) butter in a pan and fry the onions and garlic until golden brown. Add the pigeon breasts and mango. Gently fry until the breasts are sealed on both sides. Remove the breasts and reserve. Add the mushrooms to the pan with the red wine, honey, lemon juice, and salt and pepper. Stir well, cover and simmer gently for 5 minutes. Return the breasts to the pan and add the stock.

Bring to the boil, cover and simmer for 1½–2 hours. Add the Cognac.

Remove the breasts, slice thinly and arrange on a warm serving dish. Whisk the flour and ½ oz (15 g) butter into the sauce, stirring well all the time. Pour a little sauce over the sliced breasts and put the remainder in a sauce dish to serve with the meal.

Soft blue cheese potato gratin

This is a real man's dish. My husband Stuart adores it.

3–4 medium-sized potatoes
6 oz (175 g) soft blue Brie
10 fl oz (300 ml) milk
5 fl oz (150 ml) double cream
2 cloves garlic, crushed
Salt and pepper
1 tomato, sliced
2 oz (50 g) Cheddar cheese, grated
½ teaspoon mixed dried herbs

Peel the potatoes, boil them and slice into wedges. Put the Brie, milk, cream, garlic, and salt and pepper in a bowl and mix well. Put the potatoes in an ovenproof dish, pour over the Brie sauce and top with the sliced tomato, grated Cheddar and mixed herbs. Bake on the middle shelf of the oven at gas mark 6, 400°F (200°C), for 40 minutes. Remove from the oven and place under a hot grill until golden brown. Serve immediately.

Broccoli with garlic and fresh thyme steamed on a bed of glazed shallots

8-12 oz (225-350 g) broccoli,
separated into florets
3-4 shallots, sliced
2 teaspoons brown sugar
2 cloves garlic, crushed
A few sprigs of fresh thyme
1 lemon, cut into wedges, to garnish

Trim the broccoli stalks. Place the sliced shallots in a steamer, cover with the broccoli stalks and sprinkle with the brown sugar and crushed garlic. Place the fresh thyme on top. Steam for 10 minutes. Arrange the shallots and broccoli on a warmed serving dish and decorate with the lemon wedges.

Tarte aux pommes with honey and almonds baked with a cheese crust and served with a chantilly cream

We were cycling round the vineyards in the Loire valley and we got to Château Usse which looks like a fairytale castle. Opposite we found a little café where we ordered brandy and tarte aux pommes which was fabulous. When we got home I tried to re-create that dish, but adding cheese to the pastry because I love to add cheese to everything.

FOR THE PASTRY
8 oz (225 g) plain white flour, sifted
2 oz (50 g) lard
2 oz (50 g) margarine
A pinch of salt
2 oz (50 g) Cheshire cheese, grated or
crumbled

FOR THE FILLING
3-4 large cooking apples
A handful of orange and/or lemon peel
2 in (5 cm) cinnamon stick
Juice of 1 lemon
6 oz (175 g) flaked almonds
8 oz (225 g) honey
1 teaspoon mixed spice

To make the pastry, put the flour, lard, margarine, salt and 2 tablespoons water in a bowl and mix together. Roll out the pastry and use it all to line a large pie dish. Sprinkle over the cheese and bake blind at gas mark 6, 400°F (200°C), for 10 minutes.

Peel the apples and cut them into chunks. Place them in a bowl with the orange and/or lemon peel, cinnamon stick and lemon juice. Cover with hot water and leave to soak for 20 minutes. Cover the pastry crust with almonds and honey, then a layer of drained apples. Sprinkle over the mixed spice. Keep layering with honey, almonds and apples until all used up. Bake at gas mark 6, 400°F (200°C), for 45 minutes. Serve with chantilly cream (see p. 118).

The East Midlands

•

STARTER
Scotch woodcock

•

MAIN COURSE
Salmon filo parcels

•

DESSERT
Apple tart

Scotch woodcock

'A short sharp shock to begin a dinner with.'

LOYD GROSSMAN

$1 \times 1\frac{1}{2}$ oz (40 g) tin anchovies, drained
4 oz (100 g) butter
4 slices bread
4 egg yolks
5 fl oz (150 ml) double cream
Salt and pepper

Reserve a few anchovies for decoration and mash the rest with 3 oz (75 g) butter. Cut the bread into circles with a large pastry cutter and toast. Generously spread the anchovy butter over the toast and keep warm. Melt the remaining 1 oz (25 g) butter in a small heavy-based pan. Take off the heat and beat in the egg yolks, then the cream. Return to a gentle heat, stirring, until thickened. Season very lightly with salt and pepper to taste. Divide the mixture between the rounds of toast, decorate with very thin strips of anchovy and serve.

Salmon filo parcels

FOR THE PARCELS
6 oz (175 g) butter
4 pieces crystallised stem ginger, chopped
4 oz (100 g) shelled pistachio nuts, chopped
2 oz (50 g) sultanas, chopped
1 lb (450 g) tail-end fillet of salmon
4 sheets filo pastry

FOR THE SAUCE
2 tablespoons chopped fresh dill
4 tablespoons lemon juice
3 egg yolks
6 oz (175 g) butter, cut into small chunks
Salt and black pepper
A few sprigs of fresh dill, to garnish

CAROL ALEXANDER'S MENU
Fish plaits with spinach and watercress sauce, Dambuster steak, Summer fruit brûlé

JOAN BUNTING'S MENU
Goat's cheese and cherry parcels, Guineafowl with Pineau des Charentes, Rice timbales,
Carrot and courgette ribbons, Broccoli with pine nuts, Parfait Dentelles

SILVIJA DAVIDSON'S MENU
Rare poached wild salmon 'cakes' with English asparagus, Dry-spiced lamb, Stovied
potatoes, Wilted spinach salad, Rose-scented rhubarb with creamy yoghurt
and pistachios

MASTERCHEF

MARY HENDRY'S MENU
Strips of pink trout marinated like gravad lax, Chicken breast filled with piquant
seasonings in an orange and wine sauce, Baby beetroots filled with onion and celery,
Parsleyed new potatoes, Chocolate sponge medallions filled with redcurrants and
blackcurrants and chocolate cream with a currant and cassis coulis

MASTERCHEF

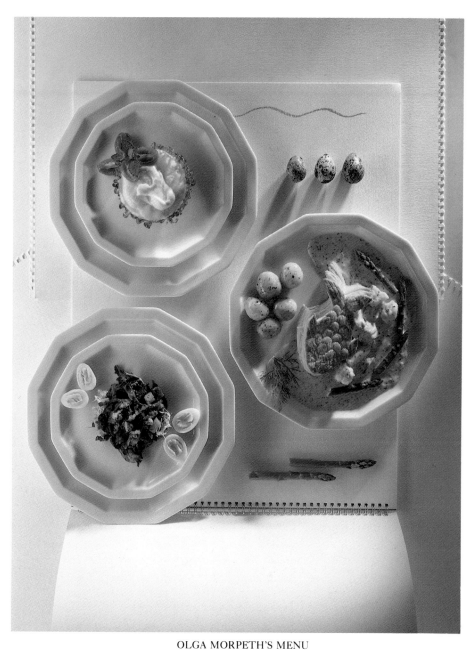

OLGA MORPETH'S MENU
Moulded warm chicken liver salad with smoked bacon and croûtons, Puff pastry
poissons with monkfish, salmon and asparagus, White chocolate mousse in caramel
baskets with glazed kumquats

MASTERCHEF

RICHARD SUTTON'S MENU
Medallions of monkfish with a sabayon of chervil, Chicken breast stuffed with a
pistachio mousseline served with two sauces, mango and watercress, Honey and whisky
ice-cream in tuile baskets

FRANCES SMITH'S MENU
Quail with mushrooms, Paupiette of salmon and julienne of vegetables, New potatoes,
Hot apple soup with cinnamon biscuits

ALISON RIDDELL'S MENU
Swiss salad with gougères, Scalloped fillets, Peppered beans, Almond meringue brûlée

Prepare the stuffing by putting 2 oz (50 g) butter in a bowl with the ginger, nuts and sultanas. Mix well. Bone and skin the salmon fillet and cut into 8 equal pieces. Melt the remaining 4 oz (100 g) butter. Lay out a sheet of filo pastry, keeping the rest covered with clingfilm. Brush with melted butter. Place a piece of salmon in the centre of the pastry, cover with stuffing, then another piece of salmon. Fold in the edges of pastry and make a parcel, brushing with melted butter each time you fold the pastry. Bake at gas mark 6, 400F (200°C), for 30 minutes.

To make the sauce, put the dill and lemon juice in a bowl over a pan of boiling water. Beat in the egg yolks, then the small chunks of butter, stirring well until all the butter has been incorporated and the sauce has thickened. Season with salt and black pepper.

To serve, place a parcel on each plate, pour some sauce beside it and garnish with a few sprigs of fresh dill. Accompany with a selection of fresh vegetables or a green salad.

Apple tart

'A saucy little pudding.'
BRUCE OLDFIELD

FOR THE PASTRY
2 oz (50 g) butter, diced
2 oz (50 g) lard, diced
8 oz (225 g) plain white flour
½ teaspoon salt
3 tablespoons ice-cold water

FOR THE FILLING
1 lb (450 g) cooking apples
2 fl oz (50 ml) Calvados
4 egg yolks
4 oz (100 g) sugar
2 oz (50 g) ground almonds
Juice of 1 lemon
2 oz (50 g) butter, melted
1 eating apple, cored and cut in rings

For the pastry, rub the fat into the flour and salt until the texture resembles breadcrumbs. Add the water and knead gently to form a dough.

To make the filling, peel, core and slice the cooking apples. Place in a pan with the Calvados and simmer until cooked. Sweeten with half the sugar, or to taste. Roll out the pastry and use it to line a 9 in (23 cm) flan dish. Arrange the cooked apples on the pastry. Beat the egg yolks, then mix in the remaining sugar, almonds, lemon juice and butter. Spoon the mixture on top of the cooked apples. Decorate with eating apple rings. Bake at gas mark 6, 400°F (200°C), for 20 minutes. Serve hot with cream.

MARY HENDRY'S MENU

STARTER

Strips of pink trout marinated like gravad lax

·

MAIN COURSE

Chicken breast filled with piquant seasonings in an orange and wine sauce

Baby beetroots filled with onion and celery

Parsleyed new potatoes

·

DESSERT

Chocolate sponge medallions filled with redcurrants and blackcurrants and chocolate cream with a currant and cassis coulis

Strips of pink trout marinated like gravad lax

This is a cheaper version of gravad lax. My father brought back something similar from Scandinavia 20 years ago and we all thought at the time that it was nicer than smoked salmon so I've been making it ever since. If you buy the trout filleted it really does save a lot of time. Also, be careful not to over-salt the trout as it will go tough very easily.

3–4 level teaspoons salt
3–4 heaped teaspoons sugar
1 teaspoon freshly ground black pepper
6–8 teaspoons chopped dill (fresh or frozen)
3–4 pink trout (preferably filleted)
2 tablespoons Greek yoghurt
1 teaspoon tomato purée
½ head Lollo Rosso lettuce, separated into leaves
Fresh dill, to garnish

Put all the dry ingredients and the dill together in a bowl and mix well, using the smaller quantities if using only 3 pink trout. Remove all the tiny bones from the trout. Place a little marinade in a shallow dish, place the trout on top and cover with the remaining dill mixture. Cover with clingfilm and refrigerate for 24 hours, basting occasionally with the juices.

Remove the trout from the marinade and pat dry with kitchen paper. Skin the trout and cut into thin strips. Mix the Greek yoghurt with the tomato purée. Place the trout on a bed of Lollo Rosso and garnish with a little yoghurt mixture and fresh dill.

Chicken breast filled with piquant seasonings in an orange and wine sauce

On the chicken breast you will find a little lump of flesh, the *filet mignon*. Take this off and put it inside the breast with the stuffing. It neatens it up and makes it look plump.

4 oranges
2 cloves garlic, crushed
2 teaspoons wholegrain mustard
½ oz (15 g) butter, softened
4 chicken breasts, skinned
7 fl oz (200 ml) fruity white wine
Salt and pepper

Finely grate the rind from 2 of the oranges, mix with the crushed garlic, 1 teaspoon mustard and the softened butter. With each chicken breast, remove the *filet mignon*, carefully make an opening on one side and insert the *filet mignon* and some of the orange and mustard paste. Gently pull the opening closed.

Squeeze the 2 grated oranges into a frying pan, stir in the remaining teaspoon of mustard and the white wine, and put on to simmer. When simmering, put in the chicken breasts, top side down. Cover and simmer gently for about 7 minutes, then turn over and cook for another 7 minutes.

While the chicken is cooking, prepare the other 2 oranges by peeling off thin strips of rind with a zester.

Remove the remaining peel and pith with a sharp knife, separate the orange segments and reserve. Place the julienne strips of orange rind in a pan of cold water and bring to the boil. Drain and refresh in cold water. When the chicken is cooked, remove from the pan and keep warm. Reduce the sauce until slightly thickened, taste and season with salt and pepper if necessary.

Dish up the chicken on to individual plates and garnish with a few orange segments and julienne strips of rind. Serve with filled baby beetroots and new potatoes cooked with mint and tossed in melted butter and chopped parsley.

Baby beetroots filled with onion and celery

---

4 baby beetroots
Safflower or sunflower oil
1 small onion, finely chopped
2–3 sticks celery, finely chopped
Salt and pepper
1–2 teaspoons paprika
1–2 teaspoons tomato purée

Trim the beetroots, cook in boiling salted water until tender and set aside. Heat a little oil in a pan and fry the onion and celery without colouring. Season with salt and pepper. Add the paprika and tomato purée to taste and cook for a few minutes.

Cut the beetroots in half, making sure that they can stand upright. (If necessary cut a thin slice off the base.) Remove the centres with a sharp-edged teaspoon and fill each one with a mound of onion and celery mixture. Line a baking tray with foil and arrange the filled beetroot halves on the tray. Bake at gas mark 3, 325°F (160°C), for about 15 minutes.

Chocolate sponge medallions filled with redcurrants and blackcurrants and chocolate cream with a currant and cassis coulis

---

This dessert is adapted from a disastrous attempt at a John Tovey recipe. The primroses I use for decoration are from a clump which was given to me when I first took my husband home to meet my parents. Needless to say they have seeded all over the place and flower in profusion from November to April. To prepare the primroses for this dessert, brush six flowers with egg white, dust with caster sugar, shake off the excess and leave to dry on greaseproof paper. If primroses are not available then you need to use something very light such as a blackcurrant leaf or any suitable flowers such as violets or pansies. You can also replace the redcurrants and blackcurrants in the sauce with any fruit. Strong sharp-tasting berries such as raspberries or tayberries seem to work best.

FOR THE SPONGE
2 size 4 eggs
1 tablespoon clear honey
1 oz (25 g) caster sugar
1 oz (25 g) wholewheat self-raising flour
2 teaspoons cocoa
1 teaspoon cornflour

FOR THE COMPOTE AND COULIS
*4 oz (100 g) fresh or frozen
redcurrants, thawed if frozen
4 oz (100 g) fresh or frozen
blackcurrants, thawed if frozen
2 tablespoons caster sugar
1-2 teaspoons arrowroot
3½ fl oz (100 ml) cassis*

FOR THE CHOCOLATE CREAM
*2 oz (50 g) luxury cooking chocolate
5 fl oz (150 ml) double cream*

FOR THE DECORATION
*Cocoa and icing sugar
6 sugared primroses (see introduction)
A few redcurrants and blackcurrants*

To make the sponge, break the eggs into a large bowl. Then line 2 Swiss roll tins with bakewell paper. Add the honey and sugar to the eggs and beat with an electric mixer until the mixture looks foamy and a lifted beater leaves a ribbon trail on the surface. Carefully fold in the sifted flour, cocoa and cornflour and place 10-11 large tablespoonfuls in the tins, spreading the mixture out a little. Bake at gas mark 4, 350°F (180°C), for about 10 minutes. When cooked, remove from the paper with a palette knife and place on a wire rack to cool.

To make the compote, put the fruit, sugar and a little water together in a pan. Simmer gently until tender but not mushy. Slake the arrowroot with a little water, stir into the compote and simmer until thick. Allow to cool.

For the chocolate cream, put the chocolate in a bowl over a pan of boiling water. Stir to melt and mix in a little double cream. Whip the remaining cream until it holds its shape, then stir in the chocolate mixture. Place in a piping bag with a large six point nozzle.

When ready to assemble, cut the sponge medallions with a plain 3½ in (9 cm) pastry cutter. Spread half the medallions with some of the cooled compote. Pipe 5 chocolate cream shells around one side of these medallions and a little in the middle. Place another medallion on top at an angle. Repeat until all the medallions are used.

To decorate, cover half of each top medallion with paper and shake a mixture of cocoa and icing sugar on the other half. Now remove the paper and shake icing sugar on the other half, covering up the cocoa powder to make a sharp line.

To make the coulis, put the remaining compote in a blender with the cassis. Whiz until smooth, and sieve, using a plastic sieve. Dilute if necessary with a little water.

Place the filled medallions on individual plates and surround with a little coulis. Arrange a sugared primrose on each filled medallion and a few redcurrants and blackcurrants on the coulis. If fresh currants are available, small sprigs could also be dipped in caster sugar and used to decorate.

PAM HOLMES'S MENU

•
STARTER
Tomato mousse
•
MAIN COURSE
Gressingham duck breasts with kumquats
Minced potatoes
Stir-fried mixed vegetables
•
DESSERT
Individual apple pies

Tomato mousse

I love this dish because lovage is one of my favourite herbs, with a flavour which is a cross between curry and celery. I grow my own lovage because it's not the sort of thing you can find in the supermarket every day of the week. If you can't find any lovage, you could actually use any other herb that you're fond of.

2 teaspoons aspic crystals
3 tablespoons powdered gelatine
4 tablespoons hot water
3 tablespoons cold water
1 × 15 oz (425 g) tin tomatoes
1 small bayleaf
1 slice onion
2 in (5 cm) stick celery
1 small slice green pepper
A squeeze of lemon juice
Salt and pepper
A pinch of sugar
1 teaspoon pesto sauce
Rind of 1 lemon
A few black olives, stoned and cut into circles
A few fresh fennel fronds
5 fl oz (150 ml) Greek yoghurt
1 tablespoon horseradish sauce
1 teaspoon finely shredded lovage
1 head frisée (or curly endive), separated into leaves
4 large prawns

Dissolve the aspic in 4 tablespoons hot water. Pour a layer of aspic into 4 ramekin dishes and allow to set. Put 3 tablespoons cold water in a small bowl and sprinkle on the gelatine. Leave to soak for 5 minutes, then stand in a saucepan of hot water to melt. Put the tomatoes, bayleaf, onion, celery, green pepper, lemon juice, salt, pepper and sugar in a blender or food processor. Whiz until smooth, sieve and add the gelatine and pesto sauce. Check the seasoning.

Cut small diamond shapes from the lemon rind and arrange decoratively on the set aspic with the black olives and fennel fronds. Gently cover with another layer of aspic and allow to set. Pour the tomato mixture into the ramekins and, again, allow to set. Mix the Greek yoghurt with the horseradish sauce and lovage.

To serve, turn out the mousses on to individual plates and garnish with the frisée, large prawns and yoghurt mixture.

Gressingham duck breasts with kumquats

Originally I cooked this recipe using chicken, so you could substitute chicken breasts if Gressingham duck breasts were unavailable. The breasts should marinate for at least 4 hours and preferably overnight.

4 duck breasts (preferably Gressingham), skinned
Seeds from 8 cardamom pods, ground
A pinch of black pepper
Juice of 2 oranges (about 8 tablespoons)
2 tablespoons olive oil
2 shallots, finely chopped
1½ (40 g) butter
10 fl oz (300 ml) duck or chicken stock
2 tablespoons Grand Marnier
8 kumquats
A few thin threads of courgette skin
Salt and pepper
A few sprigs of fresh tarragon, to garnish

Place the duck breasts in a shallow dish, sprinkle with the ground cardamom and black pepper, pressing well in with the fingers. Pour over the orange juice. Cover with clingfilm and refrigerate overnight.

The next day, drain the duck breasts, reserving the marinade, and pat dry. Heat the olive oil in a pan, and gently fry the shallots until soft. Add the duck breasts and fry for approximately 5 minutes on each side (the centre should still be pink). Remove from the pan and arrange in a serving dish.

Put the butter in the pan and melt slowly. Add the reserved marinade, the stock and Grand Marnier, and boil gently until slightly reduced and syrupy. Slice the kumquats thinly and toss in the sauce, together with the courgette threads. Season with salt and pepper and pour over the duck breasts. Garnish with a few sprigs of fresh tarragon.

Minced potatoes

I've never seen these on a menu. I like to cook them because they're slightly different from new potatoes or roast potatoes. The timing is very important. You must mince them when they are warm and if necessary you can then cover them and leave them in a warm oven, but don't let them dry out on top. The potatoes must be a waxy variety such as red Désirée or Romano.

2 lb (1 kg) waxy potatoes
Salt
2 oz (50 g) butter, melted
Fresh coriander, to garnish
A few toasted pine nuts, to garnish

Cook the potatoes in their skins in a pan of boiling salted water until just tender. While still warm, pass through the finest blade of a mincer, straight into a serving dish. Sprinkle with salt and drizzle over the melted butter. Garnish with fresh coriander and toasted pine nuts.

Stir-fried mixed vegetables

2 tablespoons grapeseed oil
3 oz (75 g) mangetout
3 oz (75 g) miniature corn on the cob
½ red pepper, de-seeded and sliced
3 oz (75 g) small broccoli florets
1 clove garlic, finely chopped
1 in (2.5 cm) piece fresh ginger, finely chopped
Salt and pepper
1 tablespoon sesame oil

Heat the grapeseed oil in a wok or frying pan. Toss in all the vegetables, together with the garlic and ginger. Fry over a high heat, stirring, for a maximum of 5 minutes. Season with salt and pepper, turn into a serving dish and sprinkle with the sesame oil.

Individual apple pies

These are based on an old Lincolnshire recipe. In the seventeenth century they would make a big pie with half a dozen apples and they would then pour beer into it, which sounds revolting, but I liked the idea of pouring something into the pies. The apples must fit snugly into the ramekin dishes or the pastry will collapse around them. The best apples to use are Cox's – cooking apples would definitely be a bit too sharp.

FOR THE PASTRY
8 oz (225 g) self-raising flour
Salt
4 oz (100 g) butter
1 oz (25 g) lard
½ oz (15 g) soft brown sugar
½ egg, beaten

FOR THE FILLING
2 oz (50 g) no-soak dried apricots, chopped
½ oz (15 g) nibbed almonds
4 tablespoons clear honey
4 tablespoons lemon juice
4 small Cox's apples
½ egg, beaten
A little sugar

TO SERVE
Clotted cream
A few amaretti biscuits or ratafias, crushed
8 fresh lemon balm leaves

To make the pastry, sift the flour and salt into a food processor or mixing bowl. Cut the fat into small cubes and add, together with the sugar. Process or mix by hand, adding the egg at the same time. Stop as soon as the ingredients are incorporated. Knead together, and refrigerate for 45 minutes.

For the filling, place the apricots and nuts in a small bowl and add 2 tablespoons honey and 2 tablespoons lemon juice. Mix well. Peel and core the apples and place 1 in each of 4 small pie dishes. Fill the centres with the apricot mixture, spreading any remaining mixture around the apples. Roll out the pastry and cover each dish, making a hole in the centre. Brush with beaten egg and sprinkle with sugar. Bake at gas mark 4, 350° F (180°C), for 15 minutes, then reduce the heat to gas mark 3, 325° F (160°C), for a further 15 minutes.

Mix the remaining 2 tablespoons honey and 2 tablespoons lemon juice into a syrup. When the pies are cooked, pour the syrup through the hole in the top. Serve with clotted cream decorated with crushed biscuits. Arrange 2 lemon balm leaves in the hole on top of each pie.

The North

KIERAN McBRIDE'S MENU

·
STARTER
Stuffed grapes with melon
·
MAIN COURSE
Chicken in vermouth with leek and watercress sauce
Mangetout
Minted new potatoes
Deep-fried cauliflower
·
DESSERT
Brandysnap baskets with a raspberry custard cream

Stuffed grapes with melon

'This gives Mae West a whole new line – not "Peel me a grape" but "Stuff me a grape"!'
ANNA RAEBURN

1 lb (450 g) black grapes
8 oz (225 g) cream cheese
3 stems chives, chopped
2 fl oz (50 ml) single cream or 3 tablespoons natural yoghurt
1 honeydew melon
½ head crisp lettuce, separated into leaves

Cut the grapes lengthways and not quite the whole way through. Remove all the pips. Put the cream cheese, chives and cream or yoghurt in a bowl and mix well. Spoon into a piping bag and fill each grape with the cheese mixture. Chill well. Use a melon baller to scoop out some melon balls and chill also. Serve the grapes and melon balls on a bed of crisp lettuce, allowing 6–7 grapes per person.

Chicken in vermouth with leek and watercress sauce

You must use double cream rather than single otherwise the sauce will curdle when you boil it. Remember to use the green part of the leek to strengthen the colour from the watercress.

4 chicken breasts
6 oz (175 g) button mushrooms, finely chopped
2 shallots, finely chopped
2 leeks, finely chopped
2 fl oz (50 ml) vermouth
Salt and pepper
2 oz (50 g) butter
A bunch of watercress
4 fl oz (120 ml) chicken stock
6 fl oz (175 ml) double cream, or to taste

Place each chicken breast on a square of foil large enough to make a parcel. Sprinkle small amounts of chopped mushroom, shallot and leek over each chicken breast. Pour about 1 tea-spoon vermouth over each chicken breast and season with salt and pep-per. Make into a parcel and seal well. Place on a wire rack over a roasting tin of water and bake at gas mark 4, 350°F (180°C), for about 25–30 minutes.

Melt the butter in a frying pan. Gently sweat the remaining chopped vegetables with a few sprigs of watercress until soft and well cooked. Add the remaining vermouth and reduce. Add the chicken stock and bring to the boil. Place the mixture in a blender and whiz until fairly smooth. Pass through a sieve into a clean frying pan. Add the cream in moderation. Warm through and reserve until required.

Unwrap the chicken parcels, removing all the chopped vegetables, and place on warmed plates. Pour some sauce over and around each chicken breast, garnish with sprigs of watercress, and serve with mangetout tossed in butter and black pepper, and minted new potatoes.

Deep-fried cauliflower

This is my mum's recipe. Everyone raved about it when she made it for dinner parties so I pinched it! It's worth experimenting by adding different flavours to the breadcrumbs such as garlic or herbs. It's also good to serve cold at parties with dips.

1 large cauliflower, broken into florets
3 eggs, beaten
4 tablespoons milk
8 oz (225 g) seasoned flour
12 oz (350 g) fresh breadcrumbs
Oil, to deep-fry

Blanch the cauliflower florets in boil-ing water for about 4 minutes. Remove and refresh under cold run-ning water. Put the eggs and milk in a bowl and beat together. Dip each floret in flour, eggwash, then breadcrumbs. Heat the oil until bubbling, deep-fry the florets for 2–3 minutes, drain well and serve.

Brandysnap baskets with a raspberry custard cream

When making the brandysnaps, never add the flour while the mixture is over the heat because the biscuits will turn out too thick and the mixture will burn more easily. Vary the flavour of the sauce and the fruit according to your personal taste, and be careful to put the brandysnap on the sauce at the last minute otherwise the bottom of the basket will get soggy.

FOR THE BRANDYSNAPS
3 oz (75 g) granulated sugar
3 oz (75 g) golden syrup
3 oz (75 g) butter
3 oz (75 g) plain white flour, sifted
1/4 teaspoon ground ginger
1 teaspoon lemon juice

FOR THE RASPBERRY SAUCE
1 lb (450 g) frozen raspberries, thawed
3 tablespoons icing sugar
1/2 tablespoon lemon juice

FOR THE CUSTARD CREAM
5 fl oz (150 ml) milk
1 egg yolk
1 oz (25 g) sugar
1/2 oz (15 g) plain white flour

TO SERVE
1 kiwi fruit, sliced
6 oz (175 g) strawberries
4 oz (100 g) cherries

To make the brandysnaps, put the sugar, syrup and butter in a pan. Melt together, then remove from the heat. Add the sifted flour, ground ginger and lemon juice and mix well. Place 4 heaped teaspoonfuls of the mixture on a greased baking sheet, spaced well apart from one another. Bake at gas mark 5, 375°F (190°C), for about 6 minutes until golden brown. Remove, leave for a few seconds, then gently lift each one off the baking sheet and place over the greased bottom of a glass tumbler. Remove when set hard.

For the raspberry sauce, blend or process the raspberries to a purée, then add the icing sugar and lemon juice. Sieve into a bowl and reserve.

For the custard cream, put the milk in a pan and warm to blood heat. Put the egg yolk and 3/4 oz (20 g) sugar in a bowl and whisk together. Sift in the flour and mix well. Add the warm milk, mix together and return to the pan. Heat gently, stirring, until thick. Pour into a small bowl, sprinkle with the remaining sugar and leave until cold. Mix in 2 tablespoons raspberry sauce and fill each brandysnap basket with the custard cream.

To serve, line 4 plates with raspberry sauce. Place a filled brandysnap basket on top of the sauce and decorate each basket with sliced kiwi fruit and whole strawberries and cherries.

OLGA MORPETH'S MENU

·

STARTER

Moulded warm chicken liver salad with smoked bacon and croûtons

·

MAIN COURSE

Puff pastry poissons with monkfish, salmon and asparagus

·

DESSERT

White chocolate mousse in caramel baskets with glazed kumquats

Moulded warm chicken liver salad with smoked bacon and croûtons

If you are unable to find any balsamic vinegar, try using sherry vinegar instead.

'Terribly butch.'
LOYD GROSSMAN

'This is a classic.'
SIMON HOPKINSON

8 oz (225 g) chicken livers
A selection of small salad leaves (e.g. rocket, oakleaf lettuce, etc.)
2 rashers smoked streaky bacon
2 slices white bread (a few days old)
Olive oil (preferably extra virgin)
3 tablespoons walnut oil
1 tablespoon balsamic or sherry vinegar
1 teaspoon wholegrain mustard
Salt and pepper
A few walnuts, roughly chopped and fried, to garnish
A few hard-boiled quail's eggs, shelled, to garnish

Pick over the chicken livers, discarding any stringy bits, then wash and dry. Wash and dry the salad leaves. Cut the bacon into strips. Remove the crusts from the bread and cut into small dice. Place a 4 in (10 cm) ring on each plate. (I use a muffin ring.) Put a selection of salad leaves in the bottom and press down. Heat a frying pan, cook the bacon strips until crisp and remove with a slotted spoon. Add a little olive oil to the pan, fry the croûtons until golden, remove and drain on kitchen paper. If the pan looks very brown, wipe it out, add a little more oil and fry the chicken livers for about 5 minutes. Return the bacon and croûtons to the pan and toss together briefly.

To make the dressing, put the walnut oil, vinegar, mustard and salt and pepper in a glass screwtop jar with a tight-fitting lid. Shake well.

To serve, spoon the chicken liver mixture on top of the salad leaves. Spoon on a little dressing. Decorate with fried chopped walnuts and hard-boiled quail's eggs. Remove the rings and serve while still warm.

Puff pastry poissons with monkfish, salmon and asparagus

I find frozen puff pastry excellent for this. When you've cut out the shapes, it's important to chill the pastry for 30 minutes.

About 1½ lb (750 g) frozen puff
pastry, thawed
1 egg yolk, beaten
A pinch of salt
5 fl oz (150 ml) double cream
1 lb (450 g) salmon fillets, skinned
2 bayleaves
12 spears asparagus, top 4 in (10 cm)
only
1 oz (25 g) unsalted butter
2 shallots, finely chopped
8 oz (225 g) boneless monkfish, cubed
5 fl oz (150 ml) Noilly Prat
10 fl oz (300 ml) fish stock
2 teaspoons tomato purée
Salt and pepper
A squeeze of lime juice
2 tablespoons finely chopped fresh dill
1 tablespoon finely chopped fresh
parsley
A few sprigs of fresh dill, to garnish

Roll out the pastry to ¼ in (5 mm) thick. Use a fish-shaped pastry cutter about 6½ in (16 cm) long by 4½ in (11 cm) wide to cut out 4 fishes. Mix the egg yolk, salt and 2 tablespoons cream together to make a glaze. Brush the pastry shapes with egg glaze, place on a dampened baking tray and refrigerate for at least 30 minutes. When ready to use, bake at gas mark 7, 425°F (220°C), for 15 minutes.

Put enough water to cover the salmon in a large pan and bring it to the boil. Put in the salmon and bayleaves. When the water boils again, cook for 1 minute, then remove from the heat and leave to cool in the water. Cook the asparagus in a pan of boiling salted water until just tender. Heat the butter in a pan and cook the shallots until soft. Add the monkfish cubes and cook over a moderate heat for 2–3 minutes until just cooked and opaque. Remove the monkfish with a slotted spoon and set aside. Add the wine, bubble up, add the fish stock and allow to reduce by half. Whisk in the tomato purée and remaining cream and reduce by half again. Season with salt and pepper and a squeeze of lime juice. Stir in the chopped fresh herbs and cooked fish, keeping the salmon in chunky pieces.

To serve, split open the puff pastry fish shapes, spoon some of the filling over the base and top with the pastry lid. Place on a warmed serving dish and spoon some of the sauce around the edges. Garnish with the asparagus and sprigs of fresh dill. Serve with new potatoes, buttered spinach or Swiss chard (depending on availability).

White chocolate mousse in caramel baskets with glazed kumquats

Try to melt the chocolate very slowly otherwise it will go stringy. The reason for poaching the kumquats in caramel is that it gives them a lovely shine as well as taking away some of the sharpness.

FOR THE CHOCOLATE MOUSSE
4 oz (100 g) white chocolate, broken into squares
1 size 2 free-range egg
1 size 2 free-range egg yolk
1 oz (25 g) caster sugar
5 fl oz (150 ml) whipping cream
1 tablespoon Grand Marnier
4 sprigs of fresh mint, to decorate

FOR THE CARAMEL BASKETS AND KUMQUATS
1 lb (450 g) cane sugar cubes
A good pinch of cream of tartar
4 oz (100 g) kumquats

To prepare the mousse, first put the chocolate in a heatproof bowl. Heat a little water in a pan, until just boiling. Remove from the heat. Place the bowl over the hot water and allow the chocolate to melt slowly. Separate the egg into 2 bowls. Add the extra egg yolk to the bowl with the first yolk. Whisk the egg white until it stands up in peaks and beat in the caster sugar until very stiff. Gently fold in the egg yolks. Whip the cream until it just holds its shape. When the chocolate has melted, remove the bowl from the pan. Allow to cool a little, fold the chocolate into the egg mixture, then fold in the whipped cream and the Grand Marnier. Refrigerate until required.

For the caramel baskets, place the sugar cubes, cream of tartar and a little water in a pan and stir to dissolve the sugar. Bring to the boil and cook until pale golden. Remove from the heat. It will continue to cook until a shade darker. Allow to cool slightly before attempting to make the baskets. Work on a piece of oiled foil. Oil 4 moulds or ramekins and line with oiled foil. Using a teaspoon, drizzle the caramel over the moulds, making sure that the base and sides up to 1 in (2.5 cm) from the base are solid caramel. Leave to harden and become cold.

Halve the kumquats lengthways and remove the pips. Add a little water to the residue of caramel in the pan, heat to dissolve the caramel, put in the kumquats and poach for 10 minutes. Leave to become cold and sticky.

Remove the caramel baskets from their moulds and carefully peel away the foil. Place on a serving dish, fill each one with mousse and top with the kumquats. Chill and serve, decorated with the mint sprigs.

RICHARD SUTTON'S MENU

·
STARTER
Medallions of monkfish with a sabayon of chervil

·
MAIN COURSE
Chicken breast stuffed with a pistachio mousseline served with two sauces, mango and watercress

·
DESSERT
Honey and whisky ice-cream in tuile baskets

Medallions of monkfish with a sabayon of chervil

I invented this recipe because whenever I've eaten monkfish at restaurants it's lacked a tanginess to complement its flavour. It could be served as a main course, but you'd need a whole monkfish tail per person. It's not cheap although if you shop in markets you can still get the fish at a reasonable price. If you find monkfish hard to get hold of, poached salmon would work equally well with this sauce.

2 egg yolks
About 6 oz (175 g) butter, melted
A few drops of white wine vinegar
1 tablespoon chopped fresh chervil
Salt and pepper
1½ lb (450 g) monkfish tail, cut into 12–16 medallions
A few sprigs of fresh parsley
A few black peppercorns
1 bayleaf
A few sprigs of fresh chervil, to garnish

Put the egg yolks in a bowl over a pan of simmering water. Gradually whisk in the melted butter until the consistency is like that of a hollandaise sauce. Add a few drops of white wine vinegar, just enough to add piquancy but not enough to make it taste vinegary. Add the chopped chervil and season with salt and pepper. Keep warm over hot water but serve as soon as possible (whisk if it starts to separate).

Meanwhile, put the monkfish medallions in a steamer over boiling water. Add the parsley, peppercorns and bayleaf, and steam for approximately 8 minutes. Serve immediately with the sauce, 3–4 medallions per person, garnished with sprigs of chervil.

Chicken breast stuffed with a pistachio mousseline served with two sauces, mango and watercress

Stuffings can often be too flavourless for my liking. This one with pistachios marries well with the chicken. If you're one of the less health-conscious types, leave on the skin and pop the breasts under the grill for the last five minutes of cooking to give a nice finish. The advantage of this dish is that the sauces can be made a couple of hours in advance and reduced a few minutes before serving.

FOR THE MANGO SAUCE
1 ripe mango, skinned, stoned and roughly chopped
A knob of butter
1 shallot, chopped
5 fl oz (150 ml) full-bodied white wine
1–2 tablespoons double cream
Salt and pepper

FOR THE WATERCRESS SAUCE
5 fl oz (150 ml) single cream
A bunch of watercress (leaves only)
Salt and pepper

FOR THE CHICKEN
4 chicken breasts (preferably corn-fed)
½ egg white
1 tablespoon double cream
2 tablespoons shelled pistachio nuts
Lime slices, to garnish

Put the mango in a blender, whiz until smooth, then strain. Melt the butter in a pan and sauté the shallot lightly, then deglaze with the white wine. Simmer until reduced by half. Add the mango purée and mix. Add the cream and reduce until slightly thickened. If it thickens too much, add a dash more wine. Season with salt and pepper.

For the watercress sauce, put the cream, 2 tablespoons water and the watercress in a pan. Simmer gently for 8 minutes, then leave to cool for a few minutes. Whiz in a blender until smooth, then strain. Return the sauce to the pan, reduce until slightly thickened and season with salt and pepper.

Trim the chicken breasts and put the trimmings in a blender with the egg white, cream and pistachios. Whiz for a few seconds, leaving the nuts slightly crunchy. Lay the chicken breasts out and spread the underside with mousseline mixture. Roll up from one end to the other, wrap each one in foil and place on a baking tray. Bake at gas mark 7, 425°F (220°C), for 15–20 minutes and serve immediately.

When ready to serve, unwrap each chicken parcel, place on an individual plate and slice across into 4–5 pieces. Pour the sauces on either side. Garnish with lime slices and serve with vegetables of your choice separately.

Honey and whisky ice-cream in tuile baskets

Although I don't have a particularly sweet tooth I love this ice-cream because the alcohol combats the sweetness of the honey. It's extremely simple to make and proves that sometimes simple dishes turn out the best. Make sure that you whisk the honey and egg yolk well to incorporate a lot of air, and mix them over a bed of ice and water to keep the mixture cool. If you prefer, you could serve this ice-cream in brandysnap cups rather than tuile baskets.

'Brilliant.'
SIMON HOPKINSON

FOR THE ICE-CREAM
2 egg yolks
5 oz (150 g) set honey (preferably clover)
5 fl oz (150 ml) double cream
1 miniature bottle whisky
A few whole strawberries, to decorate

FOR THE TUILE BASKETS
2 egg whites
4 oz (100 g) caster sugar
2 oz (50 g) plain white flour, sifted
2 oz (50 g) butter, melted
½ teaspoon vanilla essence

To make the ice-cream, whisk the egg yolks and honey together until doubled in volume. Add the cream, whisk until thick, then add whisky to taste. Put in the freezer until set.

To make the tuile baskets, whisk the egg whites until frothy. Add the sugar and whisk again until shiny. Fold in the sifted flour. Add the melted butter and vanilla essence and mix well. Grease a baking tray, then drop spoonfuls of mixture on to the tray, spreading each one into a thin circular shape. Bake at gas mark 5, 375°F (190°C), for 5–6 minutes, until the edges start to brown. Watch carefully! Using a fish slice or palette knife, loosen each biscuit from the tray and shape over a greased upturned cup or ramekin. If the biscuits start to harden before they're on the ramekins they can be softened again by popping back into the hot oven for a few seconds. When cool, fill the biscuits with ice-cream, decorate with whole strawberries and serve.

The South-East

FRANCES SMITH'S MENU

·

STARTER
Quail with mushrooms

·

MAIN COURSE
Paupiette of salmon and julienne
of vegetables
New potatoes

·

DESSERT
Hot apple soup with cinnamon
biscuits

Quail with mushrooms

2 tablespoons olive oil
1 onion, chopped
1 carrot, sliced
1 stick celery, sliced
1 clove garlic
A few sprigs of fresh marjoram or any
other herb
4 large flat mushrooms
4 fresh quail
About 2 oz (50 g) pleurote or button
mushrooms
2 large tomatoes
Salt and pepper
6 fl oz (175 ml) red wine
Frisée (or curly endive) leaves, to
garnish

Heat the olive oil in a pan, add the stock vegetables (the onion, carrot and celery), garlic and fresh herbs, and fry gently for a few minutes; allow to colour. Cut off the mushroom stalks and add to the stock pot, along with 1 pint (600 ml) water. Simmer gently. Fry the mushroom caps until just cooked, then set aside.

Spatchcock the quail (cut down the spine with a pair of scissors, open each bird out flat, and secure by weaving a skewer through it). Put any giblets in the stock pot. Steam the small mushrooms until just cooked and arrange attractively on the large mushrooms. Skin, de-seed and dice the tomatoes, putting the skins and seeds in the stock pot. Lightly oil and season the quail with salt and pepper and grill for about 5 minutes on each side. While the quail are cooking, arrange the diced tomatoes around the edge of 4 plates. Put the 4 large mushrooms on a baking sheet, ready for reheating. When the quail are cooked, cut them up and arrange each bird on a large mushroom, the leg joints underneath the breast fillets. Chop the carcasses into the stock.

Add the wine to the stock and bring to the boil, reducing to about ½ pint (300 ml). Reheat the quail and mushrooms in a very hot oven for 2–3 minutes and set on warm plates. Strain the stock and spoon over the quail. Garnish with frisée leaves.

Paupiette of salmon and julienne of vegetables

My favourite thing to cook is fish, especially salmon, because I love the colour, texture and taste. To flatten the salmon evenly, try using the side of a meat cleaver or the bottom of a saucepan.

'This is a work of art.'
GEORGE MELLY

About 8 oz (225 g) colourful seasonal vegetables (e.g. courgette, pimento, carrot, celeriac, leek and mangetout)
1 teaspoon chopped fresh coriander
1½ lb (750 g) middle cut salmon fillets
Sea salt and freshly ground black pepper
2 handfuls fresh young spinach
1 pint (600 ml) fish stock
4 fl oz (120 ml) dry white wine
10 fl oz (300 ml) double cream
A little walnut oil
About 1 oz (25 g) unsalted butter
12 sprigs of fresh coriander, to garnish

Cut the seasonal vegetables into julienne strips. Blanch for 1 minute in boiling salted water, drain, refresh under cold water and set aside. Add the chopped fresh coriander and mix well.

Slice the salmon fillets lengthways into flat escalopes, laying each one between 2 pieces of clingfilm and flattening gently with a cleaver. You may not need all the fish. Use the 4 biggest pieces for this dish. Take off the upper layer of clingfilm and season the top surface with sea salt and freshly ground black pepper. Place about a quarter of the julienne on each piece of salmon and roll up neatly. Roll the salmon in plenty of fresh clingfilm, knotting the ends and smoothing out any air bubbles. Repeat for all 4 slices. Finely shred the spinach and put in a bowl.

To make the sauce, put the fish stock in a pan and reduce until syrupy. Add the wine and reduce again. Add the cream and simmer gently. Meanwhile, immerse the fish rolls in plenty of just simmering water for 6 minutes. Take out and rest on a tea towel for 1 minute. While the fish is resting, dress the spinach with sea salt and walnut oil.

Arrange a bed of spinach in the middle of 4 warm plates. Snip open one end of each fish roll and slide off the clingfilm. Slice the untidy end off each roll, cut into 3 and arrange on top of the spinach. When the sauce has reduced to a thick enough consistency, remove it from the heat, whisk in the butter and pour round the fish. Garnish each portion with 3 sprigs of coriander and serve with new potatoes.

Hot apple soup with cinnamon biscuits

The cinnamon for the biscuits must be freshly ground.

'Delicious. The biscuits are exceptional.'
ALASTAIR LITTLE

FOR THE APPLE SOUP
1 large Bramley apple
Juice of 1 orange
Juice of ½ lemon
2 in (5 cm) cinnamon stick
2½–3 tablespoons sugar
4 Granny Smith apples
A small knob of butter
Ruby port, to taste

FOR THE BISCUITS
1½ oz (40 g) butter
1½ oz (40 g) caster sugar
1 size 2 egg white
1½ oz (40 g) plain white flour
1 heaped teaspoon freshly ground cinnamon

To make the soup, peel, core and cut up the Bramley apple. Put in a pan with water to cover, the orange juice, a piece of orange rind and the lemon juice. Add the stick of cinnamon and about 2 tablespoons sugar. Simmer until infused, then strain through muslin into a clean saucepan.

Peel the Granny Smiths and make into balls with a small melon baller. Heat a very small knob of butter and 2 teaspoons sugar in a heavy-based non-stick pan, put in the apple balls and shake and turn until caramelised. Set aside.

To serve the soup, reheat the apple juice, adding sugar to taste and port for a good pink colour. Pour into soup bowls, add the apple balls and serve with the biscuits.

To make the biscuits, first cream the butter and sugar. Then lightly whisk the egg white and beat into the mixture. Fold in the flour and cinnamon with a metal spoon. Grease but do not flour a baking sheet. Put tiny spoonfuls of mixture well spaced apart on the baking sheet and bake at gas mark 4, 350° F (180° C), for about 10 minutes or until the edges are golden brown. Cool on a rack.

GRAEME RICHARDSON'S MENU

·

STARTER
Monkfish and salmon ravioli with saffron and herb sauce
·
MAIN COURSE
Fillet of lamb in a lightly minted sauce
Carrot and asparagus mousse
·
DESSERT
Profiteroles on a purée of strawberries

Monkfish and salmon ravioli with saffron and herb sauce

Everything should be 100 per cent fresh for this, otherwise it will be awful. The sauce should be very thin, of a soupy consistency.

FOR THE PASTA
10 oz (275 g) plain white flour
A pinch of salt
3 eggs
A pinch of saffron
2 teaspoons olive oil

FOR THE FILLING
4 oz (100 g) sole fillet
4 fl oz (120 ml) double cream
Salt and cayenne pepper
4 oz (100 g) monkfish fillet
4 oz (100 g) salmon fillet
1 egg, beaten

FOR THE SAUCE
1 clove garlic
1 shallot, chopped
5 fl oz (150 ml) dry white wine
14 fl oz (400 ml) fish stock
A splash of double cream
1 sachet saffron strands
2 small courgettes
Olive oil
1–2 tomatoes, skinned, de-seeded and chopped
Salt and pepper
Chopped fresh basil, tarragon and chives

To make the pasta, sift the flour and salt into a mixing bowl. Make a well in the centre and drop the eggs in. Mix the saffron with 2 tablespoons water, then add the saffron water and olive oil to the dough. Mix well and knead for a few minutes. Divide into 4. Wrap in clingfilm and refrigerate for at least 30 minutes.

For the filling, put the sole fillet, cream, salt and cayenne pepper in a blender or food processor and whiz for 1 minute. Pass the mixture through a sieve. Finely dice the monkfish and salmon and add to the mixture. Season as necessary. Pass the pasta through a pasta-making machine until it's as thin as possible, then cut out 8 circles with a 3 in (7.5 cm) pastry cutter. Divide the fish mixture equally between 4 of the circles of pasta. Brush the edges with beaten egg, cover each one with another circle and press the edges together.

To make the sauce, put the whole peeled garlic clove in a pan with the chopped shallot and wine. Reduce until almost no liquid remains, then add the fish stock and a splash of double cream. Reduce until the liquid has the consistency of a thickish soup. Add the saffron and strain. Cut the courgettes into julienne strips and sauté in olive oil until cooked but firm. Do the same with the chopped tomato. Add to the sauce, heat through and season with salt and pepper. Add the basil and tarragon and another pinch of saffron if needed.

When ready to serve, slide the ravioli pasta parcels into boiling water and boil for 3 minutes. Divide the sauce between 4 bowls, add the ravioli and sprinkle chopped chives on top.

Fillet of lamb in a lightly minted sauce

This only works if the stock is right. It really needs a good veal stock. It's important not to overcook the lamb and, depending on its size, it sometimes needs as little as 3 minutes. I find olive oil mixed with butter is as good as clarified butter and saves a lot of trouble.

Olive oil and butter
4 fillets cut from best end neck of lamb
(bones reserved)
1 pint (600 ml) veal stock
1 small red onion, chopped
A splash of red wine
A small bunch of fresh mint, chopped
Salt and pepper

Heat some olive oil and butter in a frying pan and seal the lamb fillets until brown on all sides. Remove and set aside. Using the same pan, brown the lamb bones and add to the veal stock. Now put the chopped red onion and the red wine in the pan and simmer until reduced. Add to the stock.

When the lamb bones have been simmering in the stock for 30 minutes, strain into another pan and reduce to a sauce consistency. Add the chopped mint (reserving a little for garnish), simmer for a few minutes, strain again and set aside.

Bake the lamb at gas mark 8, 450°F (230°C), for 8–9 minutes, or until cooked but still pink inside. When ready to serve, slice each fillet into 5–6 pieces and place on a plate with the spinach-wrapped mousse. Spoon some sauce around the fillets and garnish with chopped mint.

Carrot and asparagus mousse

Season this well as it can taste bland. I don't think you need too many vegetables with the main course so I use very small ramekins.

6 oz (175 g) carrots
6 oz (175 g) asparagus, woody ends removed
2 tablespoons double cream
Salt and pepper
1 egg white, beaten until stiff
4 large spinach leaves

Cook the carrots and asparagus separately in boiling salted water until tender. Drain and allow to cool.

Put the carrots in a blender or food processor, add 1 tablespoon cream and season with salt and pepper. Whiz for a few minutes, then pass through a sieve. Fold in half the egg white and set aside. Repeat this procedure with the asparagus. Blanch the spinach in boiling water, refresh under cold water and dry.

Butter 4 tiny ramekins and line each one with a spinach leaf. Pipe or spoon a layer of carrot mousse, then asparagus mousse into each ramekin. Enclose with the flaps of spinach. Place the ramekins in a roasting tray half-filled with water and bake at gas mark 4, 350°F (180°C), for 30 minutes. Turn out and serve.

Profiteroles on a purée of strawberries

I don't make a lot of puddings, and if I do, I usually make the more traditional ones like treacle tart. However, these profiteroles look good and I think it's fun to make choux pastry. Contrary to popular belief, it's very easy to do. The secret is not to stir it too much. If you do, the fat leaks out and the pastry won't rise.

FOR THE CHOUX PASTRY
2½ oz (65 g) butter
A pinch of sugar
3 fl oz (85 ml) milk
3 oz (75 g) plain white flour, sifted with a pinch of salt
2 large eggs, beaten

FOR THE FILLING
10 fl oz (300 ml) crème fraîche
2 teaspoons vanilla-flavoured sugar
1 egg white, beaten until stiff

FOR THE CHOCOLATE SAUCE
1 tablespoon cocoa
8 oz (225 g) plain chocolate, broken into squares
½ oz (15 g) butter
Icing sugar

FOR THE STRAWBERRY PURÉE
8 oz (225 g) strawberries
Caster sugar
A few drops of lime juice
4 sprigs of fresh mint, to decorate

To make the pastry, place the butter and sugar in a pan with the milk and 4 fl oz (120 ml) water. Bring to the boil, reduce the heat and add the flour. Stir gently until the ingredients are blended and the mixture comes away from the sides of the pan. (Remember not to stir too much, as the butter may 'leak'.) Take off the heat and allow to cool slightly before adding the beaten eggs, a little at a time. The paste should now look slightly shiny. Transfer the paste to a piping bag fitted with a ½ in (1 cm) nozzle and pipe 8 small mounds on to a greased baking sheet. Bake at gas mark 4, 350°F (180°C), for 10 minutes, then reduce the heat to gas mark 2, 300°F (150°C), and leave the oven door open for a further 10–15 minutes until dry. Transfer to a wire rack and cut almost in half horizontally to let the steam out. When cool, refrigerate until required.

For the cream filling, beat the crème fraîche until fluffy. Add 3 tablespoons iced water while beating, 1 tablespoon at a time. Add the sugar, and finally fold in the stiffly beaten egg white.

To make the chocolate sauce, put the cocoa in a pan with 5 fl oz (150 ml) water. Bring to the boil, then turn down to the lowest heat and gradually add the chocolate, stirring. Finally add the butter, a little at a time, and stir until smooth.

Pipe the crème fraîche mixture into the profiteroles, put them together in a large dish and dust with icing sugar. Pour over the hot chocolate sauce and allow to set slightly before serving.

For the strawberry purée, hull the strawberries (reserving 4 whole ones for decoration) and put them in a blender. Add caster sugar to taste and whiz for a minute or so. Strain through a fine sieve and add lime juice to taste.

To serve, divide the strawberry purée evenly between 4 small plates. Carefully place 2 profiteroles on each plate, trying not to let the chocolate run into the strawberry. Halve the 4 reserved strawberries and place 2 halves on each plate. Use a small sprig of mint to resemble the strawberry stalk.

ALISON RIDDELL'S MENU

·
STARTER
Swiss salad with gougères
·
MAIN COURSE
Scalloped fillets
Peppered beans

DESSERT
Almond meringue brûlée

Swiss salad with gougères

If you can't get hold of raspberry vinegar, any fruit vinegar or lemon juice will go with the strawberries.

FOR THE SALAD
8 ripe strawberries
A little caster sugar
4 baby courgettes, about 3½ in (8.5 cm) long
2 oz (50 g) Gruyère cheese
3 oz (75 g) smoked back bacon
Sunflower oil
2 tablespoons plain yoghurt
1 teaspoon finely grated fresh ginger
2 teaspoons raspberry vinegar or lemon juice
Salt and pepper

FOR THE GOUGÈRES
1 oz (25 g) butter
4 tablespoons water
2 rounded tablespoons strong plain white flour
1 egg, beaten
1½ oz (40 g) Gruyère cheese, grated
Salt and pepper
A pinch of mustard powder

Slice the strawberries (allowing about 6 slices per person) and arrange in a ring around the plates. Sprinkle with a little caster sugar. Blanch the courgettes briefly in boiling water, then dice 3 of them and make 16 julienne strips from the remaining one. Dice the Gruyère. De-rind the bacon, cut it into fine strips and sauté in a little oil until just crisp.

To make the dressing, mix the yoghurt, ginger and vinegar or lemon juice together. Season to taste with salt and pepper, and finally add a little of the warm bacon fat and oil. Toss the diced courgettes and cheese in the dressing and spoon into the centre of each plate, adding the julienne strips and topping with a little bacon. Serve with a few small gougères.

To make the gougères, bring the butter and water to the boil in a small pan. Lift off the heat and add the flour all at once. Beat vigorously and, when smooth and glossy, beat in the egg, then the cheese, salt and pepper and mustard. Place teaspoonfuls on a damp baking sheet and bake at gas mark 6, 400° F (200° C), for about 20 minutes. Serve warm.

Scalloped fillets

---

8 fresh scallops
Juice of ½ lemon
1 × 2 lb (1 kg) Dover sole, lemon sole
or other flat fish
1 large orange
Sea salt and freshly ground white
pepper
4 thin slices white bread
2 oz (50 g) butter
1 clove garlic, crushed
1 teaspoon chopped fresh parsley
15 fl oz (450 ml) good fish stock
1 oz (25 g) flour
A little caster sugar

First prepare the fish. Trim the scallops and slice each one into 2–3 rounds. Reserve the roes. Sprinkle all with lemon juice and keep cool. Remove the 4 fillets from the fish (approximately 5 oz (150 g) each) and lay them in a buttered ovenproof dish. Cut a slice from the centre of the orange and set aside for the garnish. Thinly grate the rind of the remaining orange and squeeze. Sprinkle the juice and grated rind over the fillets. Season lightly with sea salt and freshly ground white pepper, cover and set aside.

To prepare the shells, use a 3 in (7.5 cm) pastry cutter to cut out 4 circles from the bread, and trim with scissors into scallop shapes. Mix 1 oz (25 g) butter with the garlic and parsley to make garlic butter. Spread some of the garlic butter over the shells and bake in bun tins at gas mark 6, 400°F (200°C), for about 15 minutes.

Half an hour before serving, put the fillets in a pre-heated oven at gas mark 4, 350°F (180°C), for 15–20 minutes (or microwave on high for about 5 minutes). Meanwhile, bring the fish stock to a gentle simmer. Mix 1 oz (25 g) butter with the flour to make a *beurre manié*. Gradually add the *beurre manié* to the fish stock to produce a thinnish sauce.

In a separate pan, heat the remaining garlic butter and gently cook the scallop slices and roes for 1–2 minutes. Cut the orange slice into 8 segments, sprinkle with caster sugar and slip under a hot grill for a moment to caramelise. Finally, lift the fillets on to warm plates, adding their juice to the sauce. Top the fillets with the scallops and orange segments, pour around a little of the sauce and add a 'scallop shell' filled with the roes and a bundle of Peppered beans.

Peppered beans

1 orange or yellow pepper, de-seeded
12 oz (350 g) small French beans,
topped and tailed

Cut 4 rings from the pepper, fill each
with a bundle of trimmed beans and
steam them over boiling salted water
for about 6 minutes.

Almond meringue brûlée

When I made up this recipe I was
thinking along the lines of a crème
brûlée. The sauce needs stirring
carefully and make sure that you
don't overheat it, otherwise the eggs
will curdle.

1 egg white
3½ oz (90 g) caster sugar
2 teaspoons flaked almonds
3 egg yolks
1 level tablespoon vanilla-flavoured
sugar
1 teaspoon cornflour
10 fl oz (300 ml) double cream

First make the meringues. Whisk the
egg white until it stands up in peaks,
then gradually whisk in 2 oz (50g)
caster sugar. Line a baking tray with
greaseproof paper, place spoonfuls of
meringue mixture on the tray and top
with almonds. Bake at gas mark 2,
300°F (150°C), for 1½ hours.

For the sauce, beat together the
egg yolks, vanilla-flavoured sugar and
the cornflour. Heat the cream until
warm, pour it into the egg mixture,
then strain it back into the pan. Heat
gently, stirring continuously, until it
begins to thicken and will coat the
back of the spoon. Pour the sauce into
a jug and stand in cold water to cool.

Quarter of an hour before serving,
make the caramel. Put 1½ oz (40g)
caster sugar in a pan, add just enough
water to cover and place over the
heat. When the caster sugar has dissolved completely, turn up the heat
and let it bubble until it begins to
caramelise. Meanwhile, put a
meringue in the centre of each plate
and surround with the sauce. When
the caramel is golden brown, quickly
pour a little over and around each
meringue, forming a caramel-beaded
'necklace'.

INDEX

INDEX